The

MW00935099

21 Days to Walk in the Finished Work of the Cross

THE NEW COVENANT by Reinhard Hirtler

Visit the author's website at www.braziliankidscare.org. All of the proceeds from this book go to the care of the impoverished children of Brazil and to missions.

Library of Congress Cataloging-in-Publication Data: 2017

International Standard Book Number:

E-book International Standard Book Number:

While the author has made every effort to provide accurate telephone numbers and Internet addresses at the time of publication, neither the publisher nor the author assumes any responsibility for errors or for changes that occur after publication.

First edition

17 18 19 20 21 — 987654321

Printed in the United States of America

Table of Contents

Acknowledgements

There are some people I especially want to thank because they were an important part of this book. Reini, my true son in the Lord, who lives in Poland, has specifically challenged me to study and teach about this subject of the New Covenant. Through that challenge, he triggered something in my heart that made me determined to study this topic even more intensely. I remember having some wonderful conversations with him about this subject.

Thanks to Aline, a wonderful friend, who willingly translated the manuscript for me into Portuguese.

I want to thank my wife, Debi, who encouraged me many times to preach and teach about the New Covenant. Tirelessly, she helped me to tackle this subject. She was willing to take time to type the manuscript of this book.

Thanks also to Vinícius and Camila, our friends from Rio de Janeiro, who opened their quiet and peaceful home for us in Angra dos Reis to be alone so we could type the manuscript.

To the people, who over many years, strongly resisted me as I shared my message about the New Covenant, I want to say thank you. Through your resistance you encouraged me to love selflessly and also to study this subject even more deeply.

To God, my loving and kind Father, who made such a wonderful covenant and allowed me to be a part of it.

Thanks go especially to Jesus, my amazing friend and redeemer and mediator of this wonderful New Covenant.

And last, but of course, never least, special thanks to the precious Holy Spirit, without whom I would know nothing about the New Covenant.

The work among poor children

When Reinhard und Debi Hirtler saw the terrible need among children in Brazil, their hearts broke. For the next four months, Reinhard cried every day. When they saw children living on the trash heap, on the streets, girls as young as seven years old prostituting themselves because of lack of food, they knew something had to be done.

Millions of children in Brazil live under inhumane conditions. Girls are easy prey for sexual abuse and exploitation. In 2015, they decided that something must be done in order to change this tragedy. They started an association, which is a non-profit organization, and the work among the children was born. They already purchased three houses that at this moment house 170 children.

Their long-term goal is to build 100 orphanages in Brazil to give these wonderful children a future, and a hope again and reach them with the unconditional love of God.

Every penny of the profit of this and all of Reinhard's books goes directly to this work. You can see this work as well a sign up for a monthly newsletter at www.braziliankidskare.org. We are committed to never ask anyone for money, just trust God to sustain this work. Our newsletters simply inform people what is happening with the work among these children.

Introduction

In my opinion, the New Covenant is one of the most misunderstood subjects in the Church today. Many years ago, I wrote a blog about it and triggered reactions I never expected in my wildest dreams. Some of the reactions were very strong and aggressive and did not come from unbelievers but from well-meaning Christians, church leaders, and pastors.

Generally speaking, there has been a mixture of the Old and New Covenants in the lives of Christians. Throughout most of church history, in belief and practice, the Church mixed these two Covenants, which greatly limited the expression of the life and power of Jesus Christ through her. Because the mixing of the two Covenants has been the norm rather than the exception, some of the teachings in this book might seem strange to you. If we have been accustomed to doing things in error for generations, then the right way will seem wrong to us.

I dare not think that I have the full revelation regarding the New Covenant. I do, however, have a deep desire and hunger to grow in the knowledge of it and to live fully in it. I cannot judge anyone who lives in a mix of the two Covenants because for many years in my own Christian life I did the same. All the understanding, knowledge, and revelation that I have regarding this matter, I attribute to the grace and kindness of God.

My motive for writing this book is my love for Jesus and His beautiful Church. I will purposely repeat some things in this book in order for them to become engraved deeply into your mind and heart. Paul told the Galatians, with regard to his warning against religion and Old Covenant thinking, that for him to write the same things to them was not tedious and for them it was safe (Phil. 3:1).

Please be patient as you begin to read this book because in order to fully understand the powerful truth of the New Covenant, I have to first lay a foundation and explain some basic truths, as well as explain the Old Covenant. Also, when I talk about the Covenant with Abram, I will refer to him Abraham. I am aware that when God made the Covenant with him, his name had not yet been changed. But since the Covenant is generally called the Abrahamic Covenant, I will refer to him as Abraham instead of Abram.

There is possibly nothing else that robs us of our God-given potential and the blessings of heaven, which legally already belong to us, more than a lack of understanding and experience of the New Covenant. Once our hearts truly grasp this truth we will enjoy a permanent life of blessings, victory, provision, and intimacy with the Lord. It is impossible to truly understand the New Covenant without the help of the Holy Spirit. Therefore, I ask you to start this book by praying this prayer with me:

Precious Holy Spirit, please help me to fully understand the truth of the New Covenant. Uncover any Old Covenant thinking in my heart and mind and help me to release it. I recognize my need for You and ask You to open the eyes of my heart that I may truly get hold of the message of the New Covenant. Be my Teacher from this day on. Amen.

Chapter 1

Understanding Covenant

Understanding the meaning of the word *covenant* is the key to understanding God and the Bible. Before we can understand and enjoy the fullness of the New Covenant, we must understand the meaning of *covenant* from a biblical perspective.

Covenant is the central message of the Bible. It shows us why God does and says the things He does and says. Without understanding the basics of covenant, we cannot interpret the Bible properly. Covenant is the way God relates to people.

I recently saw a T-shirt that said, "Chocolate is the answer, it doesn't matter what the question is." When I saw that, I thought, "That is also the meaning of covenant." Covenant is the answer, it doesn't matter what your question about God or the Bible is. God is a God of covenant.

Covenant or Contract?

A covenant, like a contract, is a bond that joins two parties together by obligations. Although a covenant and a contract are both bonds, the difference is very profound. Confusing these two has a huge, negative impact on a Christian's life and experience. We are not in a contract with God; we are in a covenant because God is a covenant-God—not a contract-God.

In a contract, both parties bargain with each other. They negotiate and come to an agreement which then turns into a bond, meaning they are now legally bound to each other. In a covenant, there is no negotiation. The stronger party offers the covenant to the weaker party, and the weaker can accept or reject it. I have asked many Christians if they have ever made some kind of a bargain with God, and most of them have answered, "Yes." These bargains could be things like "God, if You heal me or a loved one, I will dedicate my life to You forever"; "God, if You get me out of this mess, I promise that I will live only for You"; "God, I will give You ten percent of all of my income, so, therefore, You must bless me"; and other such similar bargains.

I have talked to many Christians who have negotiated with God at one time or another and tried to make some kind of a bargain with Him. They especially do this when they are in a very difficult, desperate, or impossible situation. That is when they think of all kinds of bargains with God. They often call these "vows," but in reality they are bargains, through which they are trying to get something from God. We cannot do this.

The reason why we cannot negotiate with God or make bargains with Him is simply because God is a God of covenant, not a God of contract. In a contract, both parties have something that the other needs. Let us say, for instance, that I want a house built. I find a builder, I negotiate the price, we come to an agreement, we both sign the contract, and now we are in a legal bond with each other. I want a house, and the builder wants the money. If I do not come up with the money, the builder is free from the bond or contract. If the builder does not build my house, I am also free from the contract and do not owe him any money.

A contract can be broken by just one party rendering it invalid because it is a mutual bond. A covenant is not a mutual bond. There is no negotiation in our covenant with God because there is nothing that we have that God needs. God is all-sufficient. Covenant is not a mutual bond. If we were to break the covenant with God, He would remain faithful and keep His end of the covenant. We would suffer the consequences outlined in the covenant, but God would still keep the covenant He made with us.

The difference between a contract and a covenant is so profound that we could say that it is like the difference between prostitution (a contract) and marriage (a covenant). People who go to prostitutes enter a contract. They want sex, and the prostitute wants money. They negotiate, agree on the price, and the contract is set. Marriage is absolutely not a contract; it is a covenant. Unfortunately, many people today see marriage as a contract. This is never how God intended or planned for it to be. Since He is a covenant-God, and marriage is a picture of Jesus and the Church perfectly united together for all eternity, marriage is a covenant. This is why God hates divorce— because He, as a covenant-keeping God, bound Himself to men in a covenant. Marriage was intended as a symbol to express His heart and character in covenant. To use our loving and amazing God for what we can get from Him moves our relationship with Him to the level of prostitution, which is a horrifying thought.

Another important difference between the two is that a contract involves only promises, while a covenant involves an oath. The writer to the Hebrews makes this very clear in Hebrews 6:13–14:

> For when God made a promise to Abraham, because He could swear by no one greater, He swore by Himself, saying, "Surely blessing I will bless you, and multiplying I will multiply you."

To promise something is a wonderful thing, but promises are often conditional. As we read through the Bible, we find that many of God's promises have conditions that we must fulfill in order to enjoy and experience His promises. Take Philippians 4:6–7 for example

> Be anxious for nothing, but in everything by prayer and supplication, with thanksgiving, let your requests be made known to God; and the peace of God, which surpasses all understanding, will guard your hearts and minds through Christ Jesus.

In these verses, we are told that the peace of God will guard our hearts and minds as we cast our cares upon Him. Not only are promises often condition, they can alsobe broken. Since a covenant is based on an oath, it is a promise. In the Bible, an oath is a very serious thing. It is considered something absolute.

Yet another difference between a contract and a covenant is that contracts exchange things or services, while covenants exchange persons. In a contract, you promise to deliver a service or a material good, and the other person delivers the money. In a covenant, you exchange your very being and surrender yourself to that other person. By His Covenant, God took "creatures" and changed them into "children." He gave Himself to us in the form of His Son, Jesus Christ. We have now become new creations of divine nature and His offspring, as told in John 1:12:

> But as many as received Him, to them He gave the right to become children of God, to those who believe in His name . . .

Jesus Is Our Covenant

In Isaiah 42:5–7, we are told that Jesus Himself has become our covenant:

> Thus says God the LORD, who created the heavens and stretched them out, who spread forth the earth and that which comes from it, who gives breath to the people on it, and spirit to those who walk on it: "I, the LORD, have called You in righteousness, and will hold Your hand; *I will keep You and give You as a covenant to the people,* as a light to the Gentiles, to open blind eyes, to bring out prisoners from the prison, those who sit in darkness from the prison house." (Emphasis mine)

It is important to understand that Jesus Himself was given to us by God as the Covenant. Without Him, there could never be a New Covenant. This was not something that God thought about after man sinned. It has always been in the heart of God. God tells us in Revelation 13:8,

All who dwell on the earth will worship him, whose names have not been written in the Book of Life of the Lamb slain from the foundation of the world.

We see that the Lamb slain from the foundation of the world was not an afterthought for God. Since Isaiah 42 tells us that Jesus, the Lamb of God, is our Covenant and that He was slain from the foundation of the world, covenant was, therefore, the original plan of God. God is not just a God of covenant, but He is also a covenant-keeping God. He will never enter into a contract with anyone—but He will always offer His covenant to whoever willingly accepts it.

Why is there so much confusion regarding the Old and New Covenants in the Church today? The devil is working very hard to make sure deception will always be manifest in the Church (2 Cor. 11:3). The problem with deception is that if we are deceived we have no idea that we have become victims of deception.

If we knew that we were being deceived, we would walk out of the deception. Next to the strategy of the enemy, I believe one of the other main reasons for confusion is that we don't understand how to read, study, and comprehend the Bible. When reading or studying it, we must apply some simple rules.

First, we must ask ourselves this question: to whom God is speaking? The Bible makes a distinction between three groups of people that God addresses and deals with differently. These three groups are the Jews, the Gentiles, and the Church of God. Look at this scripture in which we see these three groups represented. First Corinthians 10:32 says, "Give no offense, either to the Jews or to the Greeks or to the Church of God."

Second, we must understand that God deals with these three groups differently. The Jews have the Law of Moses, the Gentiles have the Law of Conscience, and the Church has the Law of Christ, or the Law of Love. Of course, God desires that all men be saved and come under the Law of Christ and the New Covenant.

Third, we must understand the different time periods. There is a dramatic difference between the time before Jesus, the time during His life on earth, and the time after His death, resurrection, and ascension. Jesus spoke several times about "That day." Only after Jesus ascended and the Holy Spirit was poured out did the Church begin to be manifest on earth. We live in the time period (or dispensation) of grace. The door of salvation is wide open for everyone. God, at this time, is not judging anyone—no person or nation. Look at 1 Thessalonians 1:10. Here we are told that the wrath of God will come after Jesus returns from heaven:

> . . . and to wait for His Son from heaven, whom He raised from the dead, even Jesus who delivers us from the wrath to come.

Finally, we must also ask ourselves this question: who is speaking? For instance, people use the Book of Job and build doctrine on parts of it, which is absurd. In the first forty-one chapters, we see that it was basically not God speaking, but rather Job and his friends. They said many things that were not in line with the heart of God. I am aware that the whole Bible is inspired by the Holy Spirit, and we need to learn from it all, but we must always distinguish between who is speaking—as well as to whom they are speaking. God Himself rebuked Job's friends in chapter 42:7 when He said,

> And so it was, after the Lord had spoken these words to Job, that the LORD said to Eliphaz the Temanite, "My wrath is aroused against you and your two friends, for you have not spoken of Me what is right, as My servant Job has."

As we learn to interpret the Bible correctly, we will have an increasing revelation of the wonderful New Covenant, enjoy it fully, and bring glory to our Lord Jesus.

Chapter 2

The Old Covenant

There are different covenants in the Bible, but the real confusion for Christians involves the Old and New Covenants. We also have God's covenant with Noah, His covenant with Abraham, and His covenant with David. Although these covenants are written in the Old Testament, they are not considered the Old Covenant.

Understanding the Old Covenant

It is absolutely impossible to fully understand and embrace everything God has for us in the New Covenant unless we first understand the Old Covenant. Therefore, we must spend some time explaining the Old Covenant in detail. In order for us to fully enter into as well as enjoy the New Covenant and experience, with all its amazing benefits, we have to fulfill a condition, which is to reject every single aspect of the Old Covenant from our beliefs and practices. We will see later that these two covenants cannot be mixed.

We must remember that a covenant is a bond; in other words, it is the way God bound Himself to us. It shows us how God deals with us and relates to us and how we must relate to Him. A lack of understanding of covenants, and especially the New Covenant, has caused Christians to relate to God on the basis of the Old Covenant. This, inevitably, will always result in a very difficult Christian life, filled with frustrations, defeat, and constant ups and downs. Such Christians constantly fight losing battles and do not seem to be able to have the victory in their lives. The sad thing is that they use Bible verses to support their bad experiences as the will of God for their lives.

Between Which Two Parties Was the Old Covenant Made?

The Old Covenant is also called the Covenant of Moses because he was the mediator of this particular covenant. A mediator is someone who stands between two parties and brings the two together. This covenant was only made between God and the nation of Israel.

This fact is very important for us to understand. Since the Old Covenant was made specifically between Israel and God, it was never supposed tbe followed by anyone else. Anyone who was not a Jew by nationality was never bound by that Covenant. I am a Gentile by nature; therefore, that Covenant was never meant for me. To live by it would be as absurd as if a Brazilian tried to live in Brazil by the rules and laws of Austria. Even if you were born Jewish, this Covenant would not apply to you anymore because it was finished in Christ. Paul tells us in Romans 10:4, "For Christ is the end of the law for righteousness to everyone who believes."

The basis of the Old Covenant was the Law, and since Christ was the end of it with His death and resurrection, the Old Covenant ended. If we could only understand this simple truth—that God bound Himself in this Covenant to a specific group of people (the nation of Israel and nobody else)—a lot of confusion would disappear from many people's lives. I am often asked by well-meaning Christians if they still need to obey certain laws of the Old Covenant.

I will answer this question in more detail later, but I want you to really grasp in your heart and mind right now that the Old Covenant was never made between anyone else except Israel and God; therefore, it is absurd for anybody else to try to live by it.

Paul fought this great battle for us and suffered much persecution for it. The religious people constantly resisted Paul and his message of grace and the New Covenant. The whole book of Galatians was written for this reason. These were people who came into the church and told the Christians that although salvation is by faith, they also had to obey some parts of the Law. Even today, I see this same problem everywhere. Preachers use very subtle words, but, in essence, they say the same things, namely, "If you want to be accepted by God, you have to do certain things"! These certain things are usually man-made rules which benefit them, their church, or their ministry. Paul used some of the strongest language in the entire Bible to resist these people. He did so because he truly understood the New Covenant and had deep revelation about the subject. Look at the following verses and notice the strong language Paul used.

I marvel that you are turning away so soon from Him who called you in the grace of Christ, to a different gospel, which is not another; but there are some who trouble you and want to pervert the gospel of Christ. But even if we, or an angel from heaven, preach any other gospel to you than what we have preached to you, let him be accursed. As we have said before, so now I say again, if anyone preaches any other gospel to you than what you have received, let him be accursed.

—GALATIANS 1:6–9

O foolish Galatians! Who has bewitched you that you should not obey the truth, before whose eyes Jesus Christ was clearly portrayed among you as crucified?

—GALATIANS 3:1

Indeed I, Paul, say to you that if you become circumcised, Christ will profit you nothing.

And I testify again to every man who becomes circumcised that he is a debtor to keep the whole law.

You have become estranged from Christ, you who attempt to be justified by law; you have fallen from grace.

—GALATIANS 5:2–4

I could wish that those who trouble you would even cut themselves off!

—GALATIANS 5:12

In Exodus 24, we find the story where God made the Covenant with the nation of Israel: Now He said to Moses, "Come up to the LORD, you and Aaron, Nadab and Abihu, and seventy of the elders of Israel, and worship from afar. And Moses alone shall come near the Lord, but they shall not come near; nor shall the people go up with him." So Moses came and told the people all the words of the LORD and all the judgments.

And all the people answered with one voice and said, "All the words which the LORD has said we will do." And Moses wrote all the words of the Lord. And he rose early in the morning, and built an altar at the foot of the mountain, and twelve pillars according to the twelve tribes of Israel. Then he sent young men of the children of Israel, who offered burnt offerings and sacrificed peace offerings of oxen to the LORD. And Moses took half the blood and put it in basins and half the blood he sprinkled on the altar. Then he took the Book of the Covenant and read in the hearing of the people. And they said, "All that the LORD has said we will do, and be obedient." And Moses took the blood, sprinkled it on the people, and said, "This is the blood of the covenant which the Lord has made with you according to all these words."

—EXODUS 24:1–8

Moses was told by God to go up on the mountain in order to receive the Covenant. God gave him the Covenant, which he then read to the people of Israel. They then had the choice to accept or reject the Covenant. As we have seen before, in a covenant there is no negotiation. God, who made the Covenant, set the terms and offered it to Israel. Israel still had the choice to accept or reject it. In verses three and seven, we clearly see that the people of Israel accepted the terms by saying, "All the words which the Lord has said, we will do," and having said that, they entered into a covenant with God:

> So Moses came and told the people all the words of the LORD and all the judgments. And all the people answered with one voice and said, "All the words which the Lord has said we will do."
>
> —EXODUS 24:3

The Basis of the Old Covenant

The basis of the Old Covenant was the Law of Moses. That Law consisted of the Ten Commandments and 603 other laws, making altogether 613 laws, which they had to obey as the basis of this Covenant.

These laws were made up of moral, ceremonial, and civil laws. They regulated every aspect of life. It told them how they needed to relate to God, how they had to interact with each other, what they were allowed to eat and not to eat, and what they could wear and not wear, etc.

The problem was not the Law, but the people; they were stubborn, refused to obey God, constantly rebelled against Him, and followed the desires of their wicked hearts. Paul tells us in the first letter to Timothy that the Law is actually good if it is used right. In 1 Timothy1:8–10, he says,

> But we know that the law is good if one uses it lawfully, knowing this: that the law is not made for a righteous person, but for the lawless and insubordinate, for the ungodly and for sinners, for the unholy and profane, for murderers of fathers and murderers of mothers, for manslayers, for fornicators, for sodomites, for kidnappers, for liars, for perjurers, and if there is any other thing that is contrary to sound doctrine . . .

The Law also regulated their lives with each other. It was an eye for an eye and a tooth for a tooth, which would still be very helpful for many people today. This is a good argument against those who say that the Law was bad. Today, corrupt people can do horrible things and have little or no consequences. Meanwhile, other people err in small things and suffer huge consequences. This part of the Law showed the fairness of God. If you knocked out somebody's tooth, they could not cut off your hand. The maximum punishment you could receive was to have your own tooth knocked out.

The Conditions of the Old Covenant

In a covenant, the conditions, as well as the consequences for not keeping the conditions, are clearly outlined. The condition in the Old Covenant was to keep all of the 613 laws perfectly, not just the Ten Commandments. We need to remember again that since a covenant is not a contract (which is a mutual bond), there were consequences for breaking the covenant, but that did not release God from His side of the covenant. Psalm 89:28–34 says,

My mercy I will keep for him forever, and My covenant shall stand firm with him. His seed also I will make to endure forever ,and his throne as the days of heaven. If his sons forsake My law and do not walk in My judgments, if they break My statutes and do not keep My commandments, then I will punish their transgression with the rod, and their iniquity with stripes. Nevertheless My lovingkindness I will not utterly take from him, nor allow my faithfulness to fail. My covenant I will not break, nor alter the word that has gone out of My lips.

Here we see the difference between a contract and a covenant beautifully illustrated. In the Old Covenant, the condition for experiencing all of the blessings promised was to keep all the Law of God. If the condition was met perfectly, then all God's blessings and promises would come upon them. These promises are specifically outlined in Deuteronomy 28 and included land, prosperity, protection, health, and many other wonderful blessings.

However, if the conditions were not met perfectly by the people (who were to keep all the laws), then all the terrible consequences, outlined in the book of the Law, would come upon them. What made the Old Covenant terrible was that it entirely depended on the people of Israel. Even though they said they would keep all that God commanded them, we know that, because of their wicked hearts, they did not; indeed, they could not.

The moment they received the Law, they broke it. When God gave Moses the Ten Commandments on the mountain and he went down to the people, he heard a lot of noise. He realized that something was not right and found the people worshipping a golden calf which they had made as an idol. God clearly said in the Ten Commandments that they should not make themselves carved images as seen in Exodus 20:2–4:

> I am the LORD, your God, who brought you out of the land of Egypt, out of the house of bondage. You shall have no other gods before Me. You shall not make yourself a carved image—any likeness of anything that is in heaven above, or that is in the earth beneath, or that is in the water

under the earth . . .

Blessings and Curses

As I have already mentioned, the blessings and curses for obeying or disobeying the commandments of God were part of the Old Covenant that was specifically made between God and the nation of Israel. Since we are not part of this Covenant, they do not apply to us who live under the New Covenant. Many Christians live in fear of Deuteronomy 28, often because they are told by well-meaning preachers that unless they obey God these curses will be part of their lives. Does that mean that it is not important to obey God? Of course, it is important, but we should not obey God for fear of curses that do not even apply to us; instead, we should obey because His love has conquered our hearts. The following two verses clearly show the blessings and the curses as the basis of the Old Covenant

Now it shall come to pass, if you diligently obey the voice of the LORD your God, to observe carefully *all His commandments* which I command you today, that the LORD your God will set you high above all nations of the earth. (Emphasis mine)

—DEUTERONOMY 28:1

But it shall come to pass, if you do not obey the voice of the LORD your God, to observe carefully *all His commandments* and His statutes which I command you today, that all these curses will come upon you and overtake you. (Emphasis mine)

—DEUTERONOMY 28:15

Chapter 3

You Have to Choose

We must understand the freedom and power of choice which God gave to man. God placed Adam and Eve in the Garden of Eden and gave them the power to choose—to eat from the tree of the knowledge of good and evil or not to eat from it. God said to the people of Israel, "I set before you life and death; you choose" (Deut. 30:19, paraphrased). It always astonishes me how people try to shift the blame for their own choices onto others. God does not accept excuses for our wrong choices since He was the One who gave us the power to choose.

Either One or the Other

Since a covenant is a bond between God and people, which shows how God relates to us and how we must relate to Him, we have to choose by which covenant we will live. One of the reasons why people mix so many Old Covenant ideas into their lives is because they do not understand that covenant always involves choice.

God is the One who offers the covenant and invites people into it, but people have to choose. You cannot live (relate to God) by two covenants at the same time and enjoy His goodness, kindness, and the blessings He has already given to you in Christ. That would be like being married to two spouses, one wonderful and one mean and terrible, and then complaining that you experience so much meanness in your life. Regarding our Christian life, we have to choose if we accept God's offer of the New Covenant or not. We cannot live by both, the Old and the New Covenants, yet so many Christians do just that. We must completely reject one and embrace the other.

As seen in the previous chapter, it makes no sense to choose to live by the Old Covenant, since it was never offered to us Christians, only to Israel. We must always remember how a covenant works—namely, by the stronger partner offering it to the weaker one. There is no room for negotiation. The only two choices the weaker partner has are to accept or to reject the covenant. This is an important truth to remember because it means that we cannot choose how to receive anything from God since He is the One who sets the terms.

As people have freedom of choice, many of them still choose to live by the Old Covenant even though it was never intended for them. Unfortunately, the consequences are devastating in their everyday lives, and God is unable to change their choice or the negative effects thereof.

The Warning of Jesus

In Luke 5:36–39, Jesus talks about the Old and the New Covenants:

> Then He spoke a parable to them: "No one puts a piece from a new garment on an old one; otherwise the new makes a tear, and also the piece that was taken out of the new does not match the old. And no one puts new wine into old wineskins; or else the new wine will burst the wineskins and be spilled, and the wineskins will be ruined. But new wine must be put into new wineskins, and both are preserved. And no one, having drunk old wine, immediately desires new; for he says, 'The old is better.'"

As we look at the context of this parable, we can clearly see that Jesus is not concerned about clothes, wine, or wineskins. This was a parable, and the words are to be understood as being symbolic. We need to ask ourselves this question: "Who did Jesus say these words to and why?" Jesus was speaking to the Pharisees, who were teachers of the Law living strictly under the Old Covenant. They tried to obey all 613 laws religiously in order to gain righteousness before God and impress their fellow men. Then they also added many of their own man-made Laws, called the tradition of the elders. These were handed down from generation to generation and carried great importance. To these religious, legalistic people, the tradition of the elders was even more important than the commandments of God. Jesus showed this in Matthew 15:1–3:

> Then the scribes and Pharisees, who were from Jerusalem, came to Jesus, saying, "Why do your disciples transgress the tradition of the elders? For they do not wash their hands when they eat bread." He answered and said to them, "Why do you also transgress the commandment of God because of your tradition?"

In verse seven, Jesus calls them hypocrites, and in verse nine, He concludes that they are teaching as doctrines the commandments of men. To these people, Jesus told the parables of the new wine and old wineskins and the new piece of cloth on an old garment. These people not only strictly lived under the Old Covenant, but they were also constantly offended by Jesus. These parables were a response to their complaining against the disciples because they were eating and drinking with sinners. Let us look at the context of the new wine / old wineskins parable to understand what Jesus was trying to say:

> After these things He went out and saw a tax collector named Levi, sitting at the tax office. And He said to him, "Follow Me." So he left all, rose up, and followed Him. Then Levi gave Him a great feast in his own house. And there were a great number of tax collectors and others who sat down with them. And the scribes and the Pharisees complained against His disciples, saying, "Why do You eat and drink with tax collectors and sinners?"

Jesus answered and said to them, "Those who are well have no need of a physician, but those who are sick. I have not come to call the righteous, but sinners, to repentance." Then they said to Him, "Why do the disciples of John fast often and make prayers, and likewise those of the Pharisees, but Yours eat and drink?"

—MATTHEW 5:27–33

Here we see an argument going back and forth between these people who lived under the Old Covenant and Jesus who came to seal the New Covenant. This parable is more serious than many people understand. Jesus came to bring the New Covenant, which was offensive to the Pharisees because it was so radically new and different. They were fasting in order to impress people and to earn something from God while Jesus and His disciples were eating with the sinners. Jesus told them that they could not mix the Old with the New. If they did, everything would be lost. Jesus represented the New, the Pharisees the Old Covenant. They still wanted the disciples and Jesus to live by the Old Covenant, but Jesus refused to. Jesus said that if you mix these two together, everything will be lost.

How does Jesus' warning apply to us today? If you implement any part of Old Covenant behavior or thinking into your life, you will lose the blessings of the New Covenant. The wineskins will burst, and everything will be lost. What was the basis of the Old Covenant? The basis was to earn the blessings of God by obeying the Law. If you do anything, whether it be fasting, giving your money, reading your Bible, serving God, praying, or any other good thing in order to gain the favor of God and deserve His blessings, you have burst the wineskin and lost the good new wine. Therefore, we have to vehemently reject every aspect of the Old Covenant.

Jesus finished this parable with an interesting statement in verse thirty-nine when He said, "And no one, having drunk old wine, immediately desires new; for he says, 'The old is better.'" How can the Old Covenant be better than the New Covenant? That is the question many people have when they read this parable. Jesus never said that the old wine is better than the new wine. Instead, He said that those who have drunk the old one do not immediately desire the new one.

This is something I see constantly. Christians who have lived under a mix of the Law and the Old Covenant find it so hard to embrace the New Covenant. Their security has been in their own works and righteousness, so their immediate reaction is to reject the new wine. Once they truly taste the amazing New Covenant, they gladly leave the old behind.

The Destruction of Self-Righteousness

In my personal opinion, the greatest sin I have ever committed in my life is the sin of self-righteousness. Self-righteousness is a typical Old Covenant behavior in which one tries to get right with God on the basis of one's behavior and performance. This is so deeply ingrained in the life of the human being that it is often hard to detect. Since it is typical Old Covenant behavior, it is like putting a new piece of cloth on an old garment. The solution for self-righteousness in the New Covenant is to receive the righteousness of Jesus Christ by faith alone.

Self-righteousness is seen for the first time even before the Law and the Old Covenant existed. In the Garden of Eden, when man sinned, their eyes were opened, and they saw their nakedness. We can see how they dealt with it and how differently God dealt with it in Genesis 3:7:

> Then the eyes of both of them were opened, and they knew that they were naked; and they sewed fig leaves together and made themselves coverings.

Before we look at this verse closely, let me remind you that in understanding the Bible and how to interpret it correctly, it is important to understand certain rules. First, there is what is called the *law of first mention*. It simply means if you want to understand anything, you must find where that topic is mentioned for the first time in the entire Bible. That first mention will offer a key to understanding what God is trying to say. Second, the Bible speaks a lot through *types and symbols*. For example, the sacrifice of a pure and perfect lamb that God demanded from His people to cover their sins was a type of Jesus Christ, the pure and perfect sacrifice for our sins.

Genesis 3:7 introduces, for the first time, the topic of fig leaves are mentioned when Adam and Eve are described as covering their own nakedness. There was no change of heart; it was just an outward covering of their own perception of what they looked like. They were naked before, but there was no shame because their hearts were pure. God's answer was to cover them with the skin of a killed animal. No matter how much we try to cover ourselves by our good works, it will not be sufficient before God. Someone innocent had to die, Jesus Christ, in order to cover our nakedness. We also see this when Jesus cursed the fig tree in Matthew 21:18–19:

> Now in the morning, as He returned to the city, He was hungry. And seeing a fig tree by the road, He came to it and found nothing on it but leaves, and said to it, "Let no fruit grow on you ever again." Immediately the fig tree withered away.

Why would Jesus curse a tree which God created? Fig trees are unique in that both mature leaves and ripe fruit appear at the same time.

There was the outward sign, but no real fruit, which is exactly what self-righteousness is—leaves, but no true righteousness. Jesus cannot accept self-righteousness because it rejects His perfect righteousness.

As we look at our own lives, is it not the biggest desire of fallen human nature that when we do something wrong and discover our own nakedness, we quickly try to compensate for it with our own good works? I remember a friend telling me that when he brought flowers to his wife, her first question was, "What did you do wrong?" She immediately thought that he had done something wrong and was trying to cover it with his good works. As sad as this sounds, it is very common in most people's lives; it just expresses itself in different forms.

Since self-righteousness is a typical expression of the Old Covenant, we have to reject it with all of our strength. What was God's solution to man's failure and nakedness? Genesis 3:21 tells us, "Also for Adam and his wife the LORD God made tunics of skin, and clothed them."

God's solution was to kill an innocent animal and cover their nakedness with its skin.

This is the first picture of the New Covenant in the Bible. Remember, covenant is a bond that defines how God deals with us and how we interact with Him. Right there, in the Garden of Eden, God clearly expressed His desire for the New Covenant. Christ covers our nakedness; He is the answer to our failures because He has become our Covenant. We do not relate to God anymore through our behaviors or good works, but only through the death of Jesus Christ! The moment we believe that God owes us anything based on our performance, we have slipped back into the Old Covenant mentality and lost all the benefits and blessings of the wonderful New Covenant.

Either All or Nothing

James tells us the same thing that Jesus told us in the parable of the wineskins, but uses different words to illustrate the same truth: we cannot mix the Law and grace—or the Old and the New Covenants. We cannot pick and choose which parts of which covenant we implement into our lives and at the same time enjoy all the benefits. The moment we add parts of the Old Covenant into our lives, the consequences are unavoidable. Let us look at the following scripture from James 2:10–11, which makes it very clear:

For whoever shall keep the whole law, and yet stumble in one point, he is guilty of all. For He who said, "Do not commit adultery," also said, "Do not murder." Now if you do not commit adultery, but you do murder, you have become a transgressor of the law.

If you choose to deserve something from God by keeping the Law, you must understand that you will need to keep the entire Law every single moment of every single day. Should you fail just one time, whether in thought or deed, you will have broken the whole Law and, therefore, will not deserve God's blessings anymore.

I was preaching in Sao Paulo when God gave me a word of knowledge regarding a destroyed knee being supernaturally restored and healed. A woman responded to that specific word of knowledge, but nothing happened after she received prayer. By the prompting of the Holy Spirit, I felt that self-righteousness was the problem preventing her from receiving her miracle. I asked her to repeat after me that she was perfectly worthy to be healed independently from her own works—being dependent only on the sacrifice of the cross. After she did that, she received her healing.

Chapter 4

The Great Confusion

It is important for us to understand the difference between the Old Testament and the Old Covenant. These two are often confused by people. Many have told me that they will never read the Old Testament—only the New Testament—because they live in the New Covenant. I love the New Testament. I enjoy reading the Gospels and the epistles of Paul, and there is nothing wrong with that. But we must understand that the Old Testament and the Old Covenant are not one and the same.

The Old Covenant is the bond that God made with Israel to determine how He would relate to them and how they should relate to Him. The Old Testament, however, is referred to as the Scriptures, and, as we know today, the entire Bible is now known as the Scriptures. The only Bible Jesus had was the Old Testament. The apostle Paul only used the Old Testament to show his understanding, revelation, and knowledge of the New Covenant.

We must love all of the Scriptures, not just the parts we like or find easy to understand. The psalmist said, "The entirety of Your Word is truth, and every one of Your righteous judgements endures forever" (Ps. 119:160). Paul said to Timothy in 2 Timothy 3:15–17,

> And that from childhood you have known the Holy Scriptures, which are able to make you wise for salvation through faith which is in Christ Jesus. All Scripture is given by inspiration of God, and is profitable for doctrine, for reproof, for correction, for instruction in righteousness, that the man of God may be complete, thoroughly equipped for every good work.

Here we clearly see how important the Old Testament is for New Covenant believers. When Paul talked to Timothy about the Scriptures and their importance in his life, he was referring to the Old Testament. When Jesus was in the wilderness, tempted by the devil, He quoted verses from the Old Testament. When Jesus was walking with His disciples on the road to Emmaus, Scripture says,

> And beginning at Moses and all the Prophets, He expounded to them in all the Scriptures the things concerning Himself.

—LUKE 24:27

The problem occurs when we confuse the Old Covenant with the Old Testament. Because of this great confusion, two things have happened. Firstly, many people have applied the Old Testament through the lenses of the Old Covenant and the Law. This has turned them into modern-day Pharisees and has wounded many people. Secondly, many people have reacted against that and thrown out the Old Testament entirely, saying that we now live in the New Covenant and do not need the Old Testament anymore. There are many reactionary theologies circling around in Christian churches. This reaction is always very dangerous, as our beliefs must be based on the Word of God and not on something negative that we have experienced. We can make the Bible say almost anything if we take things out of context and misinterpret them.

Understanding the Scriptures

If we truly want to understand the Bible, we must understand some basic truths, which I taught you in chapter 1. There are other important things which we need in order to understand the Bible which I will outline in this chapter.

The Teachings of Jesus

When Jesus walked on earth, He could not give us the full revelation of the New Covenant; He could only provide hints for us. Therefore, the mystery of the New Covenant remains hidden in the Old Testament, as well as in the gospels. Unless we are willing to search and study the Old Testament in the light of the New Covenant and with the help of the Holy Spirit, it will remain a mystery to us. This will make the Old Testament very difficult to read and to interpret. Jesus told us in John 16:12–13,

> I still have many things to say to you, but you cannot bear them now. However, when He, the Spirit of truth, has come, He will guide you into all truth; for He will not speak on His own authority, but whatever He hears He will speak; and He will tell you things to come.

These verses clearly show us that everything that Jesus taught was not everything that He came to reveal. When I discovered these verses, I began to cry out to the Holy Spirit many times, asking Him to teach me the things that Jesus wanted to say to His disciples but could not. These verses show us some very beautiful truths. There were many things that Jesus desired to say, but because the disciples lived in a period of transition between the Old and New Covenants, they were unable to understand everything.

This is why Jesus never talked about the New Covenant in clear language. He briefly mentioned it at the Last Supper when He said that the wine was the cup of the New Covenant, but He never taught about it clearly. The next thing we see in these verses is that the Holy Spirit is the One who will teach us these things. That is why I began to plead with the Holy Spirit to reveal all these things to me. Nobody can explain the New Covenant better than He does. Jesus taught many things when He walked on earth, but He did not teach about the New Covenant because it was the job of the Holy Spirit to reveal it.

The Hidden Mystery

The New Covenant, which is the only way God relates to us today, was a mystery that was hidden; nobody clearly saw it. The mystery was not revealed until after Jesus ascended into heaven and sent the Holy Spirit. Therefore, if we read the Old Testament without the clearly revealed mystery of the New Covenant, it will be harmful and even dangerous. This is how religion destroys many lives today. People read the Old Testament in the light of the Old Covenant and misinterpret and misapply everything that God said. This brings death instead of life. It creates a completely wrong picture of the God whom we serve. It will turn people either into self-righteous, modern-day-Pharisees, who are judgmental and proud, or into people who live in permanent guilt, fear, shame, and condemnation.

The Most Important Words

In my personal opinion, the most important words in the entire Bible are recorded in John 19:30, where Jesus said, "It is finished!" Everything that we read and study in the Scriptures must be interpreted through these words. Without these words, we have no salvation, no healing, no blessing, and no future in heaven. When Jesus declared these words, He declared that His work of the cross was absolute and enough. If we would only learn to read everything in the Bible in the light of these words, there would be no room for self-righteousness or religion in our lives. The only way we must relate to God is through the finished work of the cross of Jesus Christ.

The Example of the Apostle Paul

Out of all of the apostles, Paul had the greatest revelation of this mystery of the New Covenant. The New Testament was given to us to understand how to apply the mystery of the New Covenant, which was hidden in the Old Testament. The apostle Paul was willing to pay any price to defend the true gospel of grace and the message of the New Covenant. He suffered terrible persecutions and spent half of his ministry-life in prisons. The suffering was not a problem for him at all because the revelation of the New Covenant was so great in his life that it outweighed the suffering by far. When he was talking to the elders in the Church in Ephesus, he told them that he was sure that more suffering and tribulation and chains awaited him because the Holy Spirit had told him so (Acts 20:22–23). His response was the following:

But none of these things move me; nor do I count my life dear to myself, so that I may finish my race with joy, and the ministry which I received from the Lord Jesus, to testify to the gospel of the grace of God.

—ACTS 20:24

What motivated Paul to gladly suffer the most terrible persecution and hardships, which he specifically describes in the letter to the Corinthians, was not his love for God but his revelation of the gospel of the grace of God. This gospel is the New Covenant revealed. In particular, the letter to the Ephesians gives us much insight into the mystery of the New Covenant. This letter and the letter to the Galatians I have read and studied more than anything else in the Bible. It is my belief that every Christian should carefully and slowly read and meditate on the first three chapters of Ephesians. Let us look at what Paul says about this mystery in Ephesians 3:8–11:

To me, who am less than the least of all the saints, this grace was given, that I should preach among the Gentiles the unsearchable riches of Christ, and to make all see what is the fellowship of the mystery, which from the beginning of the ages has been hidden in God who created all things through Jesus Christ; to the intent that now the manifold wisdom of God might be made known by the church to the principalities and powers in the heavenly places, according to the eternal purpose which He accomplished in Christ Jesus our Lord . . .

Paul clearly said that this grace was given to him to make known what is the fellowship of this mystery, which has been hidden in God from the beginning of the ages. This has always been the purpose of God, as Paul states in verse eleven. Since the New Covenant is the eternal purpose of God, we must not read or try to understand anything in the entire Bible in any other way except through the light of this wonderful mystery, "Christ in us, the hope of glory."

The Important Prayer

As we have seen before, it is only the Holy Spirit who can truly reveal the New Covenant to us.

Even Jesus Himself was unable to do it, according to John 16:12. Since He is the only one that can give us the full revelation of the New Covenant, we need to pray a certain prayer constantly for ourselves and the people we love. I have prayed this prayer for myself several thousand times and continue to pray it. This prayer is recorded in Ephesians 1:15–21:

> Therefore I also, after I heard of your faith in the Lord Jesus and your love for all the saints, do not cease to give thanks for you, making mention of you in my prayers: that the God of our Lord Jesus Christ, the Father of glory, may give to you the spirit of wisdom and revelation in the knowledge of Him, the eyes of your understanding being enlightened; that you may know what is the hope of His calling, what are the riches of the glory of His inheritance in the saints, and what is the exceeding greatness of His power toward us who believe, according to the working of His mighty power which He worked in Christ when He raised

Him from the dead and seated Him at His right hand in the heavenly places, far above all principality and power and might and dominion, and every name that is named, not only in this age but also in that which is to come.

I have frequently sat down with pastors and leaders who complained about the people they were leading. I have told many of them that instead of complaining about their people they should diligently do what the apostle Paul did and pray this prayer fervently for their people. The apostle who had such great and outstanding revelation of the New Covenant said that he never stopped praying this same prayer for the Church in Ephesus. This prayer shows that it is the Holy Spirit who is the One who reveals the New Covenant to us.

Why do we constantly have to pray this same prayer over and over again if the work on the cross has been completed? The answer is that we have not yet had full revelation of every aspect of the New Covenant. We are not praying for God to give us certain things, which He has provided through the finished work of the cross; rather, we are praying to God to give us ever-increasing revelation through the Holy Spirit to understand every aspect of this New Covenant. I encourage you to memorize this prayer and to pray it daily.

Understanding the Teachings of Jesus

When Jesus walked the earth, the New Covenant was neither in operation nor yet revealed. Therefore, everything that we read in the Gospels we have to interpret correctly. We must ask ourselves this question: "To whom was Jesus speaking in this verse, and why did He say the things that He said?" Jesus spoke many things in response to questions which the Jewish Pharisees, who lived under the Law and Old Covenant, had asked him. These things obviously do not apply to us as New Covenant Christians. I did not say that the words and teachings of Jesus do not apply to us or that they are not important. All of His teachings have importance for us today. If we do not discern whether He was teaching or specifically addressing people under the Old Covenant, we will have a lot of confusion.

Chapter 5

Understanding the Law

Since we are under grace, do any of the Laws still apply to us under the New Covenant? That is a question many people ask. Paul tells us in Romans 6:14, "For sin shall not have dominion over you, for you are not under law but under grace." Unfortunately, I have seen this scripture misunderstood and misinterpreted. People apply this scripture in a way that causes them to live lawlessly. Recently, someone told me that since we live under grace and the New Covenant and since Jesus has removed all of our sin—past, present, and future—on the cross, in God's eyes there is no more sin. He continued to tell me that even if we do something that would have been considered sin, we do not have to confess it or be concerned about it because in God's eyes sin does not exist anymore.

This seems like a logical argument, which Paul also had to face in his day. In the very next verse of Romans 6, Paul tackles this very question, when he says, "What then? Shall we sin because we are not under law but under grace?" He continues by saying, "Certainly not!" In this chapter, I will answer many questions regarding the Law, including how it applies to us and if we still have to obey it. This is an important part of understanding the New Covenant.

When Paul said that sin has no dominion over us because we are under grace and not under Law, he compared the Old with the New Covenant. We must understand that, at times, the Old Covenant was referred to as the "Law" in the Bible because Moses gave the Law and was the mediator of the Old Covenant. Under the Law, there was no power to live free from sin because our sinful nature had not yet been dealt with. The New Covenant lifted us above the Law by destroying our sinful nature and giving us grace, which means divine ability not to sin. I talk extensively about this subject in my book *Sin*.

Obedience to the Law

The simple conclusion is that since the Law was the basis of the Old Covenant and we do not live under the Old Covenant, we also do not need to obey the Law. But, as we will see, it is not quite that simple. As we have observed in the previous chapter from James, we either need to obey all of the Law or none of it, meaning we cannot pick and choose which parts to obey and which not. If you think that the Law still applies to you, then you have to obey every single one of the 613 laws. However, as we will see later, the Bible also warns us to not be lawless.

Obtaining Righteousness

The Bible is very clear that nobody can obtain righteousness by works, which means by obeying the Law. Unfortunately, many people still come to God on the basis of keeping the Law. They feel that if they do everything right, God will now respond to them. Scripture teaches us that the only righteousness accepted by God is the righteousness that comes by faith in Christ alone. Paul says in Romans 3:20, "Therefore by the deeds of the law no flesh will be justified in His sight." We must never, for one moment, attempt to obtain righteousness before God by keeping the Law, not even the Ten Commandments. God does not enjoy our good works if they are done with the motive of gaining righteousness before Him.

Reasons for the Law

The obvious question arises, "Why then did God even give the Law?" The Law had several purposes, but at the moment I want to focus on only one. The Law was given to show us our need for Christ. Paul tells us in Galatians 3:24, "Therefore the law was our tutor to bring us to Christ, that we might be justified by faith." This scripture illustrates so wonderfully the heart of God and the New Covenant. God gave the Law and told the people that if they perfectly obeyed all of the Law they would be blessed in every possible way and acceptable before Him. One of the meanings of the word *righteous* is "to be accepted." Since no man can be accepted before God by keeping the Law, the Law served as a tutor drawing us to Christ Jesus.

It clearly demonstrated the impossibility of being acceptable before God without Jesus Christ. No matter how hard man tried, he always failed. Christ, the perfect sacrifice, made us acceptable before God even though we broke the Law a million times. Without the Law, we would have never known our need for Jesus Christ. I want to emphasize again that no keeping of any Law, whether the Ten Commandments or ceremonial or civil laws, will make us right before God.

Which Laws Do We Obey?

We do not live by the Old Testament Law, but that does not mean that we are lawless. Let me answer the question concerning which laws still apply to us today. The New Testament tells us many things that we need to do. It speaks clearly against a life of lawlessness, yet it also tells us that we are not under the Law. These seem like contradictory statements and confuse many people.

Since the Law was the basis for the Old Covenant, as we have seen, and that covenant was specifically made between God and Israel, the Law obviously does not apply to us. However, the New Testament talks about the Law of Christ, the Law of Liberty, and also the New Commandment, which Jesus gave us. The only laws that we must live by in the New Covenant are the laws which Jesus or the apostles clearly taught and enforced. However, we must understand that the application of these laws of the New Covenant is completely different. We do not obey these laws in order to gain righteousness before God, but as a response to the righteousness which we have freely received through Jesus and those we gladly follow.

Jesus Raised the Standard

The standard of the Old Testament Law was already high, yet when Jesus came, He raised that standard. Instead of saying, "Don't worry about the Law," Jesus raised the standard. For instance, in Matthew 5:27–28, we read,

> You have heard that it was said to those of old, "You shall not commit adultery." But I say to you that whoever looks at a woman to lust for her has already committed adultery with her in his heart.

What did Jesus mean when He said such radical things? We must remember that Jesus lived in the period between the Old and New Covenants. In many of His teachings, such as in the Sermon on the Mount, He gave us hints regarding how to live under the New Covenant and which laws to obey. The standard of the Law of Christ is much higher than the standard of the Law of Moses. The reason for this is the power of the New Covenant. In the New Covenant, God completely destroyed our sinful nature and enabled us to live by and obey the Law of Christ, which is also the Law of Love.

The New Commandment

Jesus said to His disciples in John 13:34,

> A new commandment I give to you, that you love one another; as I have loved you, that you also love one another.

This was something they had never heard before because the Old Covenant did not work like that. Under the Old Covenant, it was an eye for an eye and a tooth for a tooth. Suddenly, Jesus spoke of a New Commandment, which was radically different from anything they had ever heard before. This is the Law of Christ or the Law of Love by which we live in the New Covenant—not in order to gain God's favor, but because we have gained His favor. Jesus did not merely tell His disciples that the new commandment is to love one another; rather, He said it is to love one another as He loved them. They knew, after walking with Him day and night for three-and-a-half years, that He loved them perfectly. In the very same chapter, Jesus demonstrated His perfect love; this is the chapter where He washed their feet and celebrated the Last Supper with them. It is also the chapter where He announced the New Covenant to them, the Covenant of Love.

The apostle Paul, as we see in Romans 13:8, is in total agreement with Jesus regarding the Law of Love. He says a few verses later (in verse 10) that "love does no harm to a neighbor; therefore love is the fulfillment of the law." James also talks about the Law of Liberty in the New Testament. He tells us in James 1:25,

> But he who looks into the perfect law of liberty *and continues in it,* and is not a forgetful hearer but a doer of the work, this one will be blessed in what he does. (Emphasis mine)

James talks about the Law of Liberty in the context of being a doer and not just a hearer of the Word of God. James concludes that those who do the Word of God will be blessed in everything they do. If we apply the lens of the Old Covenant to this scripture, we might think that if we obey the Law of Liberty and do what God says in His Word, then He will bless us in everything that we do.

Unfortunately, that is how many Christians read and understand their Bible. James does not say anything about God blessing us. He says that those who look into the perfect Law of Liberty and continue in it will be blessed. It simply describes the result of living life right. God has already blessed us in Christ Jesus, independently from anything we will ever do. In order for us to experience and walk in all the blessings that New Covenant life should bring, we need to obey the Law of Love, which is the Law of Christ or the Law of Liberty.

Law and Lawlessness

Paul was not under the Law of Moses, neither did he live lawlessly. First Corinthians 9:19–21 tells us how Paul applied the Law of Love:

> For though I am free from all men, I have made myself a servant to all, that I might win the more; and to the Jews I became as a Jew, that I might win Jews; to those who are under the law, as under the law, that I might win those who are under the law; to those who are without law, as without law (not being without law toward God, but under law toward Christ), that I might win those who are without law . . .

In verse 21, he tells us that he is not without law toward God, but under law toward Christ. Paul did not live by any part of the 613 commandments, but he lived under the Law of Christ. His heart was captured by the wonderful truth of the New Covenant, which demonstrated the deep love God had for him. His natural response was to live under the Law of Christ, which is the Law of Love. We must always remember that the Law of Moses was actually not the problem; the problem was that man was both unwilling and unable to obey the Law of God. I will show you later in this book that God will never relate to you on the basis of any part of the Law, but only on the basis of who we are in Christ.

The Caution of Jesus

Jesus cautioned us to be aware of an attitude of lawlessness. In Matthew 7:21–24, He tells us,

> Not everyone who says to Me, "Lord, Lord," shall enter the kingdom of heaven, but he who does the will of My Father in heaven. Many will say to Me in that day,

"Lord, Lord, have we not prophesied in Your name, cast out demons in Your name, and done many wonders in Your name?" And then I will declare to them, "I never knew you; depart from Me, *you who practice lawlessness!"* Therefore whoever hears these sayings of Mine, and does them, I will liken him to a wise man who built his house on the rock. . . (Emphasis mine)

I understand that different translations of the Bible use different words at the end of verse twenty-three. The original meaning in the Greek for the word *lawlessness* is "to be without a law."[1] Jesus is telling us that just confessing Him as Lord is not good enough to enter into His Kingdom. To live as if we are without any Law and to treat sin carelessly will not bring us entrance into God's Kingdom. I am not talking about salvation, but about inheriting the Kingdom. If you want to have part in Christ's Kingdom, you must understand that following the teachings of Jesus and living by the Law of Love are vital.

The Example of the Pharisees

The Pharisees kept the civil and ceremonial Law of

Moses perfectly. They also added the Tradition of the Elders, as mentioned earlier. By doing so, they broke the moral Law of God, which is the Law of Love. Jesus told them in Matthew 12:7,

> But if you had known what this means, "I desire mercy and not sacrifice," you would not have condemned the guiltless.

What happened here that caused Jesus, once again, to confront the Pharisees? The disciples were walking through a grain field on the Sabbath. Because they were hungry, they began to pluck the heads of grain and eat. Immediately, the Pharisees complained and told Jesus that His disciples were breaking the Sabbath. Remember, the Sabbath was part of the Ten Commandments. If we had to live by the Ten Commandments, Jesus would have been a terrible example for us because He constantly broke this fourth commandment about keeping the Sabbath. Jesus responded to the Pharisees by telling them that His disciples were totally blameless before God who desires mercy.

We are all in danger of becoming modern-day Pharisees who keep parts of the Law of Moses, or even worse, some man-made Laws, but show no mercy. This is an attitude we must reject and not allow to be a part of our lives. I have met countless Christians who have left their churches because of this very attitude. Their leaders applied the Law harshly instead of showing any mercy and living by the Law of Christ, which is the Law of Love.

Law or Invitation

One revelation, which transformed my life, was that the laws of the Old Covenant turn into invitations in the New Covenant. In the Old Covenant, holiness was a law; in the New Covenant, it turned into an invitation. God invites us to share in His holiness and live holy as He is holy. I remember when God said to me that if I would remove all distractions from my life first thing in the morning and not turn on my phone, look at any emails, or interact with people before I have spent time with Him and interacted with Him for a good while, then the anointing, miracles, and authority that I walk in would increase greatly. I experienced one of the greatest battles of my life because I turned it into a law. I got up every morning with the attitude that "I must not" turn on my phone and check my messages or emails before I spent time with the Lord. Then one day, the Lord told me that He never gave me a law to obey, but t hat He invited me into a life of greater anointing, miracles, and authority. This changed everything because instead of obeying a law, I just took His invitation.

Endnote

1. *anomia,* "lawlessness"; Strong's #458; http://biblehub.com/greek/458.htm; accessed 19 June 2017.

Chapter 6

Was the Old Covenant Good Enough?

Asking if the Old Covenant was good enough almost seems like a silly question, but it is a legitimate and important one. If it were clear, no Christian would ever live by any part of the Old Covenant. But as I will show you later in this book, most Christians regularly mix parts of the Old Covenant into their lives; especially when it comes to the area of money, giving, tithing, offerings, and material blessings, etc. We base our beliefs and practices much more on the Old Covenant than on the New Covenant, the words of Jesus, or the teachings of the apostles. The way we pray also usually has more Old Covenant patterns, beliefs, and behaviors in it than New Covenant practices. The Church, in general, has been an expert in twisting and misusing Bible verses to support what they want to believe.

The Bible gives us a clear answer to the question concerning whether the Old Covenant was good enough or not, which is, simply, "No." Why was the Old Covenant not good enough? Was it not God who made it for His people? The Old Covenant depended on the performance of the people. Since the people were imperfect and were unable to obey God's Law perfectly all the time, the Old Covenant did not and could not work. Man had a sinful nature because of Adam's sin; therefore, even the best of men, like David and Moses, failed under the Old Covenant. In the New Covenant, Christ brought the solution by destroying that very sinful nature so that man would not be a slave to sin anymore. We who live under the New Covenant are still able to choose to sin, but we do not have to sin anymore. This is amazingly good news!

The Better Covenant

Because the Old Covenant failed, God had to make another covenant. I would remind you, again, that covenant is a bond between God and man and shows how God relates to man and how man relates to God. God passionately loves us and wants to live in an intimate relationship with us. He also wants us to have an abundant life, so He had to find a way for Him to relate to us and for us to relate to Him that would work perfectly; therefore, He made the New Covenant. The Bible calls the New Covenant a better covenant as we see in

Hebrews 7:22: "By so much more Jesus has become a surety of a *better covenant*" (Emphasis mine).

Just as the Old Covenant depended on man, so the New Covenant depends on Jesus Christ. In this scripture, we are told that Jesus became *the surety*, which means *the guarantee*, of a better covenant. If we only understood this one verse and its full meaning, we could do nothing but rejoice all day in the goodness of our God. God bound Himself to us, and the guarantee of this love-relationship is not our performance, but our beloved Jesus Christ and His finished work on the cross. We must, with all that is within us, stop relating to God based on our performance. Unfortunately, Jesus has been limited to the role of our Savior when in reality He is so much more. He is the One who eternally guarantees that our relationship with God will always be perfect.

I am so passionately in love with Jesus—not just because He saved me, but also because I understand that I have a guarantee that is absolute. Because of the New Covenant, which Jesus guaranteed, God relates to me in a radically new way. I am deliberately giving you hints of the wonder of the New Covenant here to make your mouth water for what is coming later in this book.

Since Jesus is the guarantee of the New Covenant, and covenant denotes how God relates to us, we can conclude that God never relates to us based on our weaknesses, our past, our attempts to please Him, or our works, but only on the finished work of Jesus Christ. I have to keep reminding you that a covenant is not a contract. When God made the Covenant with us through Jesus Christ, He never entered into a contract with anybody; He eternally bound Himself to us, and because of His perfect righteousness and faithfulness, He can never be released from this bond. The only way God can ever relate to us is through the finished work of the cross and because of who we are in Christ Jesus.

Better Promises

Another reason the Old Covenant was not good enough was because the promises were limited and very conditional. Hebrews 8:6 tells us,

> But now He has obtained a more
> excellent ministry, inasmuch as He is
> also Mediator of *a better covenant*,

which was established *on better promises.* (Emphasis mine)

What are the better promises? We have to remember that the writer to the Hebrews compares the Old and the New Covenants. We are told that the promises of the New Covenant are better than the ones under the Old Covenant; therefore, we need to look at them to see how they are better. There are too many better promises to put into this book; therefore, I will only show you some of the promises of the Old Covenant and how they are better under the New Covenant.

Under the Old Covenant, sins were covered, but never totally removed. Hebrews 10:4 says, "For it is not possible that the blood of bulls and goats could take away sins." The people under the Old Covenant had to continually bring sacrifices for their sins. There was a constant awareness of sin and personal sinfulness. Under the New Covenant, however, sin is completely removed as we see in Hebrews 8:12:

> For I will be merciful to their unrighteousness, and their sins and their lawless deeds I will remember no more

What a beautiful New Covenant promise we are given here! Our sin is not only covered for a period of time, but it has been completely removed forever from our lives and replaced with Christ's perfect righteousness.

I heard a story about a prophet who was ministering in a church. He began to prophesy over various people, including a couple. As he turned to the wife, he began by saying, "And regarding that terrible sin that you have committed . . ." Then he paused and was quietly contemplating something. It was obvious that the Holy Spirit had inspired him to say what he had just said regarding a terrible sin. Now it seemed that he could not hear the voice of the Spirit anymore. Then he opened his mouth and continued to say, "I asked the Lord, 'Lord, what about that terrible sin?' and the Lord replied, 'I do not remember.'" The woman broke down in tears of joy as she was perfectly released from all guilt from her past. Oh the glory of the New Covenant!

The promises of the Old Covenant were not good enough in that they were only of an earthly nature, which included health, protection, provision, and so forth. When Hebrews tells us that we have a better covenant with better promises, it means that in the New Covenant all of our natural things are provided for—and on top of that, we have many other promises of a spiritual and eternal nature. These promises include the death of our sinful nature, justification by faith, sanctification as a free gift from God, total redemption, and an eternally secure salvation. Paul told us in Galatians 2:20,

> I have been crucified with Christ; it is no longer I who live, but Christ lives in me; and the life which I now live in the flesh I live by faith in the Son of God, who loved me and gave Himself for me.

This scripture shows something that was absolutely impossible under the Old Covenant. Under the New Covenant, with the better promises, Christ Himself expresses His life through us. Romans chapters six through eight speaks of the wonderful victory we have over sin in the New Covenant. Look at Romans 6:1–2:

> What shall we say then? Shall we continue in sin that grace may abound? Certainly not! How shall we who died to sin live any longer in it?

Paul starts the epistle to the Corinthian church with a wonderful view of how God sees His children. In 1 Corinthians 1:2, he tells us,

> To the church of God which is at Corinth, to those who *are sanctified* in Christ Jesus, called to be saints, with all who in every place call on the name of Jesus Christ our Lord, both theirs and ours . . . (Emphasis mine)

Paul addressed them as the ones who are sanctified because they are in Christ Jesus. This was absolutely impossible under the Old Covenant. He told the Corinthians that in the New Covenant that we are totally new creations and made perfectly righteous in Jesus Christ. None of that was possible under the Old Covenant.

> Therefore, if anyone is in Christ, he is a new creation; old things have passed away; behold, all things have become new.
>
> —2 CORINTHIANS 5:17

> For He made Him who knew no sin to be sin for us, that we might become the righteousness of God in Him.
>
> —2 CORINTHIANS 5:21

Another reason the Old Covenant was not good enough was because man had no direct access to God. They constantly needed a mediator who first brought sacrifices for himself and then for the people. Paul tells Timothy in his first letter, "For there is one God and one Mediator between God and men, the Man Christ Jesus" (1 Tim. 2:5).

Under the New Covenant, every person has direct access to God Himself and can take hold of everything that they need. The Most Holy Place was a place into which nobody except the High Priest could enter—and that only once a year. It was where the presence of the Most Holy God was on earth, and sinful man could not enter before that presence. As the High Priest entered once a year with a sacrifice, the people anxiously waited to see if God accepted that sacrifice. It was not a good covenant at all. When Jesus died on the cross, that thick curtain separating the Most Holy Place was torn from the top to the bottom as we are told in Mark 15:38: "Then the veil of the temple was torn in two from top to bottom."

The last reason the Old Covenant was not good enough was because God then lived in a man-made temple. The presence of God was a visitation, not something permanent, while in the New Covenant it is a habitation, meaning that God permanently lives inside of us. I do not like it when people say that they go to the house of the Lord. I equally dislike it when people invite the presence of the Lord into their meeting. These are Old Covenant thought-patterns, and the Old Covenant was not good enough. Let me show you two scriptures that show this very clearly:

> To them God willed to make known what are the riches of the glory of this mystery among the Gentiles: which is Christ in you, the hope of glory.
> —COLOSSIANS 1:27

> Do you not know that you are the temple of God and that the Spirit of God dwells in you?
> —1 CORINTHIANS 3:16

Look at the beauty of these two verses: Christ has taken permanent residence in us through the Holy Spirit. Having seen these truths, how anybody can still desire to live under the Old Covenant is a mystery to me. We are clearly told in Hebrews 8:7 that the Old Covenant was not good enough: "For if that first covenant had been faultless, then no place would have been sought for a second."

Chapter 7

Religion Distorted the Nature of God

It is my conviction that religion is an invention of Satan. When I say religion, I do not mean the different beliefs or aspects of Christianity; I mean approaching God with an Old Covenant mentality, based on works. If we try to relate to God based on the Law, we have fallen into religion. One of the worst problems with religion is that it completely distorts the nature of God. That has always been the strategy of the enemy since the beginning of creation. If we study the original sin in the Garden of Eden carefully, we will find out that the strategy of the devil was deception. He deceived Eve into believing that God was not as kind and generous as He really is. One of the big problems in not understanding the New Covenant and the finished work of the cross is that we believe in a God that is actually different from the God of the Bible.

The Kindness of God

There is only one God. He is amazingly kind and wonderful, and He passionately loves all men.

Because people have read the Bible from the perspective of the Law instead of the finished work of the cross, they have entered religion instead of a living relationship with this wonderfully kind God. Let me show you through the Bible how wonderful the God we serve is. In Hebrews 8, we see God's motive for establishing a New Covenant:

> Because finding *fault with them,* He says: "Behold, the days are coming, says the LORD, when I will make a *new covenant* with the house of Israel and with the house of Judah—not according to the covenant that I made with their fathers in the day when I took them by the hand to lead them out of the land of Egypt; because they did not continue in My covenant, and I disregarded them, says the LORD." (Emphasis mine)
> —HEBREWS 8:8–9

In this verse, the Lord tells us that the problem was not the Old Covenant but the people. Look at this verse; it says, "Because finding fault with them . . ." Then the writer concludes that it was the people who did not continue in His covenant. God could have had the attitude that since the people caused the problem, it was entirely their fault, so they were the ones who would need to find a way to fix it. He could have told them that it was their sinfulness and rebellion that was the problem, and He could have said, "I told you how to relate to Me. Now just do it." But instead of having this attitude, God goes out of His way to make a New Covenant with man. This is one of the greatest demonstrations of the kindness of God. Once we understand that this was in His heart from the foundation of the world, we will be overwhelmed with joy.

Recently, I was meditating on Psalms 139:17–18, where it says,

> How precious also are Your thoughts to me, O God! How great is the sum of them! If I should count them, they would be more in number than the sand; when I awake, I am still with You.

The thoughts of God toward you are not mean or angry; they are precious. The word *precious* means "highly valued" and "esteemed." The thoughts that God has about you are not only highly valued and esteemed, they are also so numerous that you could never count them. David was a man who was familiar with the desert.

I can imagine that, as he began meditating about the goodness of God and then looked around himself in the middle of the desert where there was nothing but sand, he had an overwhelming revelation about the kind thoughts of God toward him which were comparable with the amount of sand he saw.

There Is Only One God, and He Is Amazingly Wonderful!

Since religion distorts the nature of God, it is important for us to remove all religious filters when we approach God or His Word. Some people have the idea that there are two gods—the God of the Old Testament and the God of the New Testament. The problem is not that God presented Himself differently in the Old Testament than in the New; the problem is that the devil, through religion, has twisted the nature of God in our minds and hearts, and, therefore, we have perceived either two different gods or a God who changed in the New Testament. However, we are told in Malachi 3:6 that God never changes: "For I am the LORD, I do not change; therefore you are not consumed, O sons of Jacob." If we can only learn to read the Bible without our religious filter, we will discover the most amazing and kind God in the Old as well as the New Testament.

How you see God—His nature and His character—will determine how you relate to Him and also how you think He relates to you. Since we filter everything we hear through our hearts, we must make sure that our hearts are not clogged up with religious beliefs, which will create fear, self-righteousness, condemnation, judgmentalism, and the like. On top of that, it will either turn us into people who are convinced that we are terrible sinners or into modern-day Pharisees—both of which are horrible things.

God's Glory Is His Character and Nature

There is a wonderful narrative in Exodus 33:17–19 where Moses expresses his deep desire to see the glory of God:

> So the LORD said to Moses, "I will also do this thing that you have spoken; for you have found grace in My sight, and I know you by name." And he said, "Please, show me Your glory." Then He said, "I will make all

My goodness pass before you, and I will proclaim the name of the LORD before you. I will be gracious to whom I will be gracious, and I will have compassion on whom I will have compassion."

Moses asked to see God's glory to which God responded in an interesting way. He told Moses that He would make His goodness pass before him and that He would proclaim the name of the Lord. God never told Moses that he could not see His glory; rather, He told him that He would reveal His glory by revealing His name.

In the Hebrew culture, name always gave identity; it spoke of the nature and character of a person. People have different ideas about the glory of God. Usually, it is some strange, abstract, and supernatural thing that needs to manifest itself in order for them to believe that they have seen the glory of God. In this passage, we are told that God's glory is His nature and character, which is displayed in His goodness. Let us look at the glory of God revealed here. This passage so beautifully illustrates how people often read the Old Testament through the lens of the Old Covenant; by doing so, they totally twist the nature and character of God.

God's Glory Revealed

As God passed by Moses in Exodus 34:5–7, we see His character revealed in seven attributes, which expressed His glory:

> Now the LORD descended in the cloud and stood with him there, and proclaimed the name of the LORD. And the LORD passed before him and proclaimed, "The LORD, the LORD God, merciful and gracious, longsuffering, and abounding in goodness and truth, keeping mercy for thousands, forgiving iniquity and transgression and sin, by no means clearing the guilty, visiting the iniquity of the fathers upon the children and the children's children to the third and the fourth generation." So Moses made haste and bowed his head toward the earth, and worshiped.

It is quite astonishing to me how people who read the Bible with an Old Covenant mentality do not see the kindness of God throughout the

Old Testament. As you study ancient and modern church history, you will find out that nobody was ever significantly used by God who did not see the true kind and wonderful nature of God in the Old Testament.

It has always been God's desire, since before the foundation of the world, to live in a loving, caring, and intimate relationship with man. He has always desired that we relate to Him based on His true character and not on the distorted character that religion has portrayed. If our eyes can be opened to see God's glory, we will do nothing else but surrender to Him and worship Him. As we walk through these seven hidden attributes, I want you to remember that this is God describing Himself. Religion has lied to us when it tried to convince us that God is an angry God.

The Seven Attributes that Show God's Glory

In Exodus 34:6–7, God begins to reveal His wonderful character and nature to Moses. As we go through theses character attributes, I will tell you what their original meaning is in the Hebrew so you can truly grasp the glory of God.

The first thing that God says is that He is merciful. This means to have compassion or tender mercy. Right there, in the middle of the Old Testament, with people who lived under the Old Covenant, God showed them what He was really like. We must remember that Jesus is the perfect representation of the God that we cannot see (Col. 1:15). As you read the Gospels, you will see a compassionate Jesus, who tenderly cared about the weak, the sick, sinners, the rejected, women, and children. He was so compassionate that in His greatest times of need He did not care about Himself but about others.

The second attribute that reveals God's glory is that He is gracious. This is a very strong Hebrew word, and it is very difficult to translate into our language. The best we can do is to say that it means to be kind, friendly, and to show favor. I want you to pause and think about any idea of God that you have had by reading the Bible through the lens of religion. God has never been any other God than the one that He Himself has said He is. He will always be kind to you, He will always be friendly, and He will always go out of His way to show you His favor.

The third attribute that shows the glory of God is that He is longsuffering. This word means to be patient, slow to anger, and not easily provoked. Can you see how the devil has distorted the character of God? Many churches preach about a God that is so angry that He is always trying to find a way to release His anger upon the people. God Himself declared this not to be true.

Next, God describes Himself as abounding in goodness. This means to have much kindness and tenderness. Again, as you read through the Gospels, you will see this characteristic clearly displayed in the life of Jesus. He was so kind and tender that people who were rejected by society were "magically" drawn to Him. Mothers pushed through the crowds with their little children so that He could touch them and bless them. Prostitutes wept at His feet because they were overwhelmed by so much kindness and tenderness. Sinners, like tax collectors who were hated by society, willingly surrendered their lives to Him and followed Him. Our God is a God of kindness and tenderness. That is His glorious nature. If your heart does not believe in the tenderness of God, you will not be able to relate to Him the way that He desires you to.

The fifth of the seven attributes that God announced to Moses was that He is a God of truth. This word in the original Hebrew means to be faithful or reliable.[1] God is absolutely faithful and will always do what He promises if we dare to believe Him. Many people try to believe in the Word of God or the promises of God without having seen His glory, meaning His character. If your heart is not convinced that God, by nature, is good, kind, and reliable, then you will not have the faith to believe in His promises. Faith is not something technical; it is to connect ourselves to God's glory.

The sixth and penultimate attribute is that He keeps mercy for thousands. The word for *mercy* here is the same in the original Hebrew as was used for attribute number four, *goodness*.[2] The question arises—why would God give Himself the same attribute twice? The answer is clear. Both of these attributes have another word added to them. The first time God says that He is abundant in goodness. The word *abundant* is an adjective and means "ample, a great plenty" or "a multitude." The second time God adds a verb and a number. He says that He keeps mercy for thousands. The original meaning is that He carefully guards His tenderness and kindness toward us forever and ever.[3] The meaning of the word *thousand* in the numerology of the Bible means an endlessly long time. In simple words, God is saying here, "It is My glory to carefully watch over you and make sure that I am always kind and tender toward you."

The seventh and last attribute that God revealed to Moses is that He is forgiving. God said that He forgives iniquity, transgression, and sin. The meaning of *forgiving* is to pardon, to lift away, or to overlook. God here describes His amazing glory by telling us the things that He chooses to pardon, to lift away from us, and to overlook. These three things that God chooses to forgive are progressive. *Iniquity* means perversity, guilt, or depravity. *Transgression* means to be rebellious, which speaks of an attitude. *Sin* comes from a root word meaning to miss the mark, but it always involves a deliberate action. God declares that it is His glory to pardon our perversity, our rebellion, and even our deliberate actions against Him. I have heard it said that God does not forgive deliberate sin. I did not know there was any other kind of sin. We choose to sin, and God chooses to forgive. Such is His glorious nature. I consider it something so beautiful that, right there in the middle of the Old Testament with a rebellious people, God shows how good He really is.

Paul quotes the prophet when he says in Romans 10:21, "But to Israel he says: 'All day long I have stretched out My hands to a disobedient and contrary people.'" Again, we see the amazing nature of God who can never be stopped from loving us!

The Seeming Contradiction

As we read that passage, I deliberately left out the last part until now. In Exodus 34:7, where God describes His glorious character, He continues with the following statement:

> . . . by no means clearing the guilty, visiting the iniquity of the fathers upon the children and the children's children to the third and the fourth generation.

I have heard this statement quoted out of context many times by Christians to justify the mess in their lives. They say that there must be some sin that their father, grandfather, or great grandmother committed, and that now God is visiting their iniquity upon them and judging them for the sin of their ancestors. What a terrible

Old Covenant theology! In Christ, all ancestral curses are gone, and all things have become new.

Let us look at this apparent contradiction, which in reality is not a contradiction at all. God clearly showed us, by describing Himself in seven astonishing attributes, that He is compassionate, friendly, patient, not easily provoked, tender, reliable, and unconditionally forgiving. Look at the seventh attribute, which says, "Forgiving iniquity and transgression and sin." Right after God says that, He adds this statement: "By no means clearing the guilty, visiting the iniquity of the fathers upon the children and the children's children to the third and the fourth generation."

How can God first say that He is so kind and forgiving, and then immediately add that He will by no means clear the guilty? If we, by our free will and choice, choose to reject this amazing God—His kindness and forgiveness—then there is nothing left except the Law by which we must be judged. God never wants anybody to experience His wrath, which His holy nature demands to be released against sin. The only thing God ever wants us to experience is His mercy, kindness, goodness, and forgiveness. If we, however, choose to reject His kindness, then with a broken heart, He has to watch as we experience the consequence of our terrible choice, which is judgment.

But wait—there is another beautiful part to this story. God says He will by no means clear the guilty, and since He already settled that He is kind, tender, and forgives everything, that means there are no more guilty people before Him unless they reject His outstanding love and forgiveness. There is nobody who needs to be guilty in the eyes of our loving God; all can be forgiven. Can you see how religion and the reading of the Bible with an Old Covenant lens have distorted the picture of our lovely God and made Him out to be an angry, punishing God, which He is not?

There are two ways of rejecting God's kindness and forgiveness: one way is by deliberately declaring that we do not want to receive it, which no Christian would ever do. The other way is much more subtle; it is by self-righteousness, wherein we try to earn God's kindness, goodness, or forgiveness by our own merits. Since His glory can only be received as a free gift, if we try to deserve it, then we have rejected it.

Endnotes

1. *emeth*, "firmness, faithfulness, truth"; Strong's #571; http://biblehub.com/hebrew/571.htm; accessed 19 June 2017.

2. *checed*, "favour"; Strong's #2617; http://biblehub.com/hebrew/2617.htm; accessed 19 June 2017.

3. *natsar*, "to watch, guard, keep"; Strong's #5341; http://biblehub.com/hebrew/5341.htm; accessed 19 June 2017.

Chapter 8

Comparing the Two Covenants

There are many wonderful, direct comparisons between the Old and the New Covenants. I want to show some of them to you for three reasons: firstly, that you may reject every Old Covenant mentality; secondly, that you may fully embrace every aspect of the New Covenant; and thirdly, that you may clearly understand that the New Covenant is not a better continuation of the Old Covenant as some teach, but a radically different and new way in which God relates to us.

The Radical Difference

The difference between the Old and New Covenants is not like an upgrade, but a radical make-over. Things have changed so radically under the New Covenant that people who have related to God on the basis of the Old Covenant usually find it hard to fully embrace the New Covenant.

What Do They Depend On?

I have already mentioned this, but I want to make sure that you truly understand this important truth, since it is the most radical difference between these two covenants. What do these two covenants depend on? The Old Covenant depended on man keeping the Law while the New Covenant depends on faith in the finished work of Christ alone. This is such a radical difference because it also means that Christ kept the Law for us so that we could be delivered from the curse of the Law. Look at these two scriptures:

> Now therefore, *if you will* indeed obey My voice and keep My covenant, then you shall be a special treasure to Me above all people; for all the earth is Mine. (Emphasis mine)
> —EXODUS 19:5

> . . . by so much more Jesus has become a surety of a better covenant.
> —HEBREWS 7:22

Under the Old Covenant, you had to obey the Law in order to be God's special treasure. Under the New Covenant, where everything depends on believing that Christ sealed this covenant, we are His special treasure simply because we are in Christ. Remember, covenant is how God relates to us. No matter what we do, Christ sealed the covenant for us; this is why God relates to us through the finished work of His Son alone, which now makes us the Father's special treasure, independently from what we do. How can this truth alone not make us want to jump up and down for joy all day long? The Creator of the universe, who is all powerful, yet filled with these wonderful seven attributes which we have seen, has decided that from now on, you and I are His treasure, and this is the only way He will ever relate to us. He never expects us to relate to Him in any other way.

As I write this, I am sitting on an airplane from Johannesburg, South Africa, on my way to Lusaka, Zambia. I am really tired from having traveled for almost 24 hours now. I am experiencing two wonderful things. One is that I can hardly contain myself for the joy exploding in my heart as I am writing about this incredible New

Covenant truth. On this flight, there is also a very obviously gay flight attendant. Naturally speaking, homosexuality is something that totally grosses me out. Yet, as I am writing about this amazing aspect of the New Covenant, I am experiencing one more wonderful thing: my heart is filled with the love and compassion of God for this man. I began to pray for him for God's amazing love to reach him. Once his heart is conquered by that love, he will be so satisfied that he will need no other perverted human love.

Externals versus Internals?

The Old Covenant focused on external things, while the New Covenant focuses on internal things. In the Old Covenant, it was all about outward behavior, while in the New Covenant, it is all about the heart. It is interesting that under the Law the intentions and motives of the heart were not the focus; instead, the focus was on external behavior. Under the New Covenant, God is not requiring a change of behavior without a change of heart, which is a work of His grace. The Spirit of God creates a new heart in New Covenant believers. The word that is used for *transformation* in the New Covenant (Rom. 12:2; 2 Cor. 3:18) is the same word that the English word *metamorphosis* comes from, which does not speak of a make-over but of a complete, radical change.

Bondage and Freedom

Bondage and freedom are two totally opposite words. The Old Covenant, of course, brought bondage, while the New Covenant brought freedom, which we see in the following scriptures.

> Stand fast therefore in the liberty by which Christ has made us free, and do not be entangled again with a yoke of bondage.
>
> —GALATIANS 5:1

> And you shall know the truth, and the truth shall make you free.
>
> —JOHN 8:32

> Therefore if the Son makes you free, you shall be free indeed.
>
> —JOHN 8:36

We need to understand that there is no freedom from sin under the Old Covenant; it can only be experienced under the New Covenant.

Perfection and Imperfection

No matter how hard we try, under the Law we can never become perfect before God. Many people who struggle with perfectionism do not understand that there is absolute freedom from it under the New Covenant as Christ Himself becomes our perfection. Being made perfect is as effortless as letting go of your compulsive perfectionism and surrendering it to God in simple faith, believing and declaring that God looks at you and is satisfied with you because He sees you perfect in Christ.

> . . . for the law made nothing perfect; on the other hand, there is the bringing in of a better hope, through which we draw near to God.
>
> —HEBREWS 7:19

> Are you so foolish? Having begun in the Spirit, are you now being made perfect by the flesh?
>
> —GALATIANS 3:3

The problem with the Galatians was that they entered into the New Covenant by faith and then began to mix elements of the Old Covenant into their New Covenant life. Paul said it was foolishness to try to become perfect under the Old Covenant. I love Colossians 1:28:

> Him we preach, warning every man and teaching every man in all wisdom, that we may present every man perfect in Christ Jesus.

Paul gives us several differences between the Old and the New Covenant in 2 Corinthians 3. Please understand that the chapter specifically deals with comparing these two covenants. I would strongly advise you to read the whole chapter to get a good picture. In verse five, we see that under the Old Covenant, the ability came from oneself, while under the New Covenant, it comes from God:

> Not that we are sufficient of ourselves to think of anything as being from ourselves, but our sufficiency is from God . . .
>
> —2 CORINTHIANS 3:5

The word in the original Greek for *sufficient* means ability.[1] Under the Old Covenant, everything depended on a person's own ability, while in the New Covenant, it all depends on God's ability. That is why we are more than conquerors (Rom. 8:37) and can do all things (Phil. 4:13) under the New Covenant. In 2 Corinthians 3:6, we see that the old one kills while the new one brings life:

. . . who also made us sufficient as ministers of the new covenant, not of the letter but of the Spirit; for the letter kills, but the Spirit gives life.

There is no life under the Old Covenant. The saddest and most miserable people I have encountered in my whole life were not people who had difficult circumstances, but people who lived under the bondage of the Old Covenant and religion. They exist, but there is no expression of an abundant life. Paul continues his comparison in verse nine by telling us that the old brings condemnation while the new brings righteousness: "For if the ministry of condemnation had glory, the ministry of righteousness exceeds much more in glory" (2 Cor. 3:9).

Condemnation is a terrible thing. People who live under condemnation suffer great internal pain. Scripture tells us that under the New Covenant we are free from all condemnation (Rom. 8:1). Mental institutions are filled with people who are filled with guilt, which is an expression of condemnation. If you struggle with guilt, shame, fear, and condemnation, you most likely are trying to relate to God on the basis of the Old Covenant. Only under the New Covenant is there freedom from it through the righteousness of Christ.

More Radical Differences

Throughout the Bible, we see many more radical differences between the Old and New Covenants. Hebrews 10:4 and 7:25 tell us that the old one is powerless to save while the new one saves us to the uttermost. It is very sad to meet Christians who have no assurance of their salvation.

> For it is not possible that the blood of bulls and goats could take away sins.
>
> —HEBREWS 10:4

> Therefore He is also able to save to the uttermost those who come to God through Him, since He always lives to make intercession for them.
>
> —HEBREWS 7:25

The original meaning of the word *uttermost* means "perfectly" or "completely."[2] Under the New Covenant, our salvation is absolutely completed and guaranteed through Christ Jesus. There was no inheritance under the Old Covenant, just reward or punishment. Under the New Covenant, we are guaranteed an eternal inheritance, which nobody can ever take away from us.

> For the promise that he would be the heir of the world was not to Abraham or to his seed through the law, but through the righteousness of faith.
>
> —ROMANS 4:13

> And for this reason He is the Mediator of the new covenant, by means of death, for the redemption of the transgressions under the first covenant, that those who are called may receive the promise of the eternal inheritance.
>
> —HEBREWS 9:15

Many Christians are afraid to be confronted by an angry god. This, of course, is a mentality from the Old Covenant. People who lived under the Law had to fear the anger of God, while people under the New Covenant are saved from the wrath of God. Look at these two beautiful Bible verses:

> . . . because the law brings about wrath; for where there is no law there is no transgression.
>
> —ROMANS 4:15

> Much more then, having now been
> justified by His blood, we shall be
> saved from wrath through Him.
>
> —ROMANS 5:9

The people of Israel lived in constant fear of experiencing the anger of God. In the New Covenant, Christ experienced the anger of God on the cross even though He never sinned. Therefore, we never have to fear the anger of God because His anger has been appeased. Many Christians pray for the mercy of God in their lives. As I will show you in a later chapter, that is a prayer that we do not need to pray. Under the Old Covenant, there was absolutely no mercy; under the New Covenant, there is complete mercy, which has been given to us. Therefore, we do not need to ask for it again. This perfect mercy has been demonstrated to us in Christ Jesus.

> Anyone who has rejected Moses' law
> dies without mercy on the testimony
> of two or three witnesses.
>
> —HEBREWS 10:28

> For I will be merciful to their
> unrighteousness, and their sins and
> their lawless deeds I will remember
> no more. —HEBREWS 8:12

There is a deep need inside every person to be justified. Whenever we are caught doing something wrong, the usual reaction is to justify our actions. We do not like to live with unresolved guilt and inner conflict. The apostle Paul, as well as great reformers throughout church history, paid a high price to defend the doctrine of justification by faith alone. Under the Old Covenant, there was absolutely no justification. Under the New Covenant, however, there is perfect justification. Christ's perfect righteousness has been imparted to us, and we now have His righteous nature, independently from our own works. We must understand that if we seek to be justified by works and the Old Covenant we will also lose our justification the moment we have committed the smallest sin because we will have rejected righteousness by faith alone. The following two scriptures show clearly how radically different the Old and New Covenants are in this aspect:

> . . . knowing that a man is not justified by the works of the law but by faith in Jesus Christ, even we have believed in Christ Jesus, that we might be justified by faith in Christ and not by the works of the law; for

by the works of the Law no flesh shall be justified.

—GALATIANS 2:16

Therefore let it be known to you, brethren, that through this Man is preached to you the forgiveness of sins; and by Him everyone who believes is justified from all things from which you could not be justified by the law of Moses.

—ACTS 13:38–39

It has always been the desire of God for us to live a life of absolute abundance. When the Bible talks about the Christian life under the New Covenant, it uses a very specific Greek word, *zoe,* which means an absolute fullness of life, a life that is active, vigorous, and blessed. This is the life that every Christian should experience. We must remember that this life can only be experienced if we fully live under the New Covenant. The following verses show us that there is no true life under the Law in the Old Covenant:

Is the law then against the promises of God? Certainly not! For if there had been a law given which could have given life, truly righteousness would have been by the law.

—GALATIANS 3:21

It is the Spirit who gives life; the flesh profits nothing. The words that I speak to you are spirit, and they are life.

—JOHN 6:63

The thief does not come except to steal, and to kill, and to destroy. I have come that they may have life, and that they may have it more abundantly.

—JOHN 10:10

I have shown many radical differences in this chapter between the Old and New Covenants, so I want to summarize it all with the following statements: instead of the people's "we will do," which was their response under the Old Covenant when they received the Law, the New Covenant promises to make us perfect in every good work because God works in us. It is no longer by human effort, but has been accomplished by the finished work of Christ. We just enter into it by faith alone. It is not us working for Him, but rather

Him working in us. This can only be experienced through the blood of the Everlasting (New) Covenant, which Jesus shed on the cross.

When I was in my late teens and starting to preach and work as a pastor, I was very stressed. I felt the pressure of the ministry and the expectations of God and the people. I had to preach many times a week and was always very nervous. I always prayed very intensely and asked God to help me. One day, God told me that was not a good prayer. I was confused and wanted to know why it was not. God quickly responded that, with that mentality, I was doing the work, and He was helping me. He then told me to pray like this: "Use me, Lord." I quickly understood the difference: one was me working with His help, and the other was surrendering to the finished work of the cross so that He could work through me. What a release that was. *"It is finished!"*

Endnotes

1. *hikanos,* "sufficient, fit"; Strong's #2425; http://biblehub.com/greek/2425.htm; accessed 19 June 2017.

2. *pantelés,* "all complete, entire"; Strong's #3838; http://biblehub.com/greek/3838.htm; accessed 19 June 2017.

Chapter 9

Three Totally New Things

The New Covenant, as announced by the prophet Jeremiah, brought three totally new things that were unheard of before. These three things were so radically different, especially to the minds of the Jews, that they constantly resisted Jesus who came to announce and bring this New Covenant. The clearest revelation regarding the New Covenant was given to the apostle Paul. Even Peter, who walked with Jesus for three-and-a-half years, still mixed some Old Covenant behavior into his life after the death and resurrection of Jesus. When God wanted Peter to go to the house of a Gentile (in Acts 10), He had to first deal with some of Peter's Old Covenant mindsets. Let me paraphrase the story.

Cornelius, a Roman Centurion, who was a very religious man but not yet saved, gave money to the poor and prayed to the God whom he did not yet personally know. An angel appeared to him, telling him that he needed to send men to bring Peter to his house. Meanwhile, the apostle Peter was up on a roof praying. It is important to understand that Peter had already preached in Jerusalem where three thousand people had gotten saved. He was already part of the New Testament and New Covenant Church. The Old Covenant thinking was deeply ingrained in his heart, but God was determined to get it out of him in order to fulfill His purpose. God wanted him to preach the gospel to a Gentile, who is included in the New Covenant. But because Peter was not willing to do that due to his lack of understanding of the New Covenant, God had to use an extraordinary method.

The first thing we notice in verse ten was that God deliberately waited until Peter was hungry. As the old saying goes, "The way to a man's heart is through his stomach." The Bible says that when he was hungry, and while they were preparing the food, he fell into a trance. In this trance, he clearly saw heaven opened and a great sheet, bound at the four corners, coming down right in front of him. That great sheet was filled with all kinds of animals that a Jew under the Old Covenant was not allowed to eat. That alone would have been radical enough, but then a voice said to Peter, "Rise, Peter. Kill and eat!"

Let us recap what God did. First, He waited until Peter was hungry. Then God put him into a trance, showed him a vision that totally violated his beliefs, and on top of that, told him to do something he had been told all his life was forbidden (by God Himself) to do. Even in his hungry state, Peter replied, "Not so, Lord, for I have never eaten anything common or unclean." The Old Covenant was so deeply ingrained into his heart that he even resisted the Lord Himself. God did not quit, but rather repeated the scenario three times.

While Peter was pondering what God could possibly be trying to say to him, the people that Cornelius had sent arrived at the house where Peter was staying. Peter knew he had to go with them because the Holy Spirit had told him to, but God had to do yet another radical thing to make sure that Peter was fully convinced of the New Covenant. When Peter arrived at Cornelius' house and was preaching the gospel to them, the Holy Spirit fell on those Gentiles even before they were baptized. Up until that point, something like that had never happened before, nor has it been recorded elsewhere in Scripture. It even violated

Peter's own sermon on the day of Pentecost when he said that the people first had to repent and be baptized, and then would receive the gift of the Holy Spirit (Acts 2:38). Peter used this experience later in Acts 15 to prove the validity of the New Covenant.

Paul was so determined to defend the New Covenant that he was even willing to confront the great apostle Peter to his face as seen in Galatians 2:11–12:

> Now when Peter had come to Antioch, I withstood him to his face, because he was to be blamed; for before certain men came from James, he would eat with the Gentiles; but when they came, he withdrew and separated himself, fearing those who were of the circumcision.

The three totally new things that had never happened before were declared by the prophet Jeremiah in 31:31–34:

"Behold, the days are coming, says the LORD, when I will make a new covenant with the house of Israel and with the house of Judah—not according to the covenant that I made with their fathers in the day that I took them by the hand to lead them out of the land of Egypt, My covenant which they broke, though I was a husband to them," says the LORD. "But this is the covenant that I will make with the house of Israel after those days," says the LORD: "I will put My Law in their minds, and write it on their hearts; and I will be their God, and they shall be My people. No more shall every man teach his neighbor, and every man his brother, saying, 'Know the LORD,' for they all shall know Me, from the least of them to the greatest of them," says the LORD. "For I will forgive their iniquity, and their sin I will remember no more."

The first thing we see is that God would write His Law on the hearts and minds of the people.

"But this is the covenant that I will make with the house of Israel after those days," says the LORD: *"I will put My law in their minds, and write it on their hearts."* (Emphasis mine)

Under the Old Covenant, the Law of God was handed to Moses, and Moses had to teach the people. He was the one who had to instruct them and tell them how to live their lives. This is an area that few leaders have understood. Over and over again, I meet people who are convinced that they have to control the behaviors of their brothers and sisters by rules and regulations. I believe this is because we have not fully understood and believed in the New Covenant. God is the One who declared that in the New Covenant He Himself will put His Law into the hearts and minds of the people.

Let me tell you two true stories that illustrate how the New Covenant works in this aspect. One of them is from a pastor that I have known for more than 35 years, and the other one is from my own experience.

A young man got saved and started attending the church of my acquaintance, whose church had meetings on Sunday mornings and evenings. The young man had the habit of going to the cinema every Sunday night. After he got saved, he asked the pastor if he could still go to the movies on Sunday nights. The pastor, who is a firm believer in the New Covenant, refused to tell him what to do. The new Christian kept pressuring him to tell him what he should do, but the pastor still refused. Finally the pastor told him, "Take the Lord to the cinema with you." Is it not strange that most people prefer the Law rather than being directed by the Lord through the Law written in their own hearts?

The young man went to the cinema and asked for two tickets. The lady at the counter asked him if he was with his girlfriend, but he replied, "No." The lady asked who the second ticket was for, but he refused to answer her question. Eventually, he got the two tickets for two numbered seats next to each other. As he sat down at the cinema, he turned to the seat next to him and said, "Jesus, let's watch the movie together. I hope you enjoy it." After ten minutes, he realized that Jesus did not want to be there, and he left the cinema. From that day on, he was in the service on Sunday nights.

The second story is from my own experience when I was pastoring a local church about thirty years ago. Over a period of a few months, many young people, who had been deeply involved in various sins, got saved. Those people had never been to a Christian church in their lives. One of them was a young lady who had lived a very sensual life and loved partying. On one of her first Sunday meetings she was dancing very sensually during the time of worship, all the way in the front of the building with clothes that were very inappropriate, flashing her butt and her boobs. A member of our church came to me and said that I had to stop her from such behavior in the service. I refused to do that, standing fast in my belief in the power of the New Covenant. It was not very long before the way she dressed and behaved changed.

The second totally new thing that has never before happened is written in Jeremiah 31:34. It says that everyone will have an intimate knowledge of the Lord:

"No more shall every man teach his neighbor, and every man his brother, saying, 'Know the LORD,' for they all shall know Me, from the least of them to the greatest of them," says the LORD. For I will forgive their iniquity, and their sin I will remember no more."

What a wonderful New Covenant promise: everybody shall know the Lord personally and intimately. One of the deepest longings of the human heart is for intimacy. Man was never created to live in isolation, but in intimate relationships. Before sin came into the world, Adam and Eve lived in an intimate relationship with God. Under the New Covenant, this intimacy has been restored.

I remember early in my ministry when I woke myself up because I was speaking in my sleep out loud. I kept repeating the same words over and over again which were, "Thank You, Lord, that I don't have a religion, but a relationship." This part of the New Covenant is connected to the first promise. If you know somebody personally and intimately, you will also know what pleases them. If the Church could only learn to walk in this aspect of the New Covenant by faith, people would be more easily drawn to the Lord through her. We must vehemently reject the belief that some people have more favor with God or that He listens to their prayers more than to others'. I believe this is a very evil, religious, and Old Covenant concept because it defies the work of the cross. So many times people have told me that they wish they had such an intimate relationship with the Lord as I have. My heart weeps for everyone who does not live intimately with the Lord. My dearest friend, it is a New Covenant promise that everybody shall know the Lord. You must believe that this is part of the New Covenant, simply desire it, and by faith develop intimacy with the Lord. You are as close to Him as you want to be.

The third totally new thing that we see in the New Covenant is freedom from guilt. As we also see in Jeremiah 31:34, God will remove all guilt from the lives of His people:

> "No more shall every man teach his
> neighbor, and every man his brother,
> saying, 'Know the LORD,' for they
> all shall know Me, from the least of
> them to the greatest of them," says
> the LORD. "For I will forgive their
> iniquity, and their sin I will
> remember no more."

God declares that He will not remember their sin anymore. Guilt will destroy any relationship between two people. It will cause people to hide things from each other and to keep secrets. It will trigger fears, which are very destructive in a relationship. God declares in the New Covenant that there is no more memory of the sin that was committed in the lives of His children. God's Laws in our hearts and minds, an intimate knowledge of the Lord, and freedom from guilt were never known under the Old Covenant and are new privileges under the New Covenant.

Chapter 10

The Blood Covenant

God's covenant with Abraham is different from the Old Covenant because it was a covenant that was based on faith alone; it was also considered a blood covenant. In the Abrahamic Covenant, we see the mystery of the New Covenant. It is important for us to clearly understand what happened here in order to fully grasp what happened in the New Covenant. Without understanding the Abrahamic Covenant, it will not be possible to truly understand the New Covenant.

Christ is hidden in the entire Old Testament, and we must make sure that we find Him there. For this reason, we must read the whole story in Genesis 15:1–21 very carefully. Please do not rush through these verses; read them very slowly and carefully:

> After these things the word of the LORD came to Abram in a vision, saying, "Do not be afraid, Abram. I am your shield, your exceedingly great reward." But Abram said,

"Lord GOD, what will You give me, seeing I go childless, and the heir of my house is Eliezer of Damascus?" Then Abram said, "Look, You have given me no offspring; indeed one born in my house is my heir!" And behold, the word of the Lord came to him, saying, "This one shall not be your heir, but one who will come from your own body shall be your heir." Then He brought him outside and said, "Look now toward heaven, and count the stars if you are able to number them." And He said to him, "So shall your descendants be." And he believed in the LORD, and He accounted it to him for righteousness. Then He said to him, "I am the LORD, who brought you out of Ur of the Chaldeans, to give you this land to inherit it." And he said, "Lord GOD, how shall I know that I will inherit it?" So He said to him, "Bring Me a three-year-old heifer, a three-year-old female goat, a three-year-old ram, a turtledove, and a young pigeon." Then he brought all these to Him and cut them in two, down the middle, and placed each piece opposite the other; but he did not cut the birds in two. And when the vultures came down on the carcasses, Abram drove them away. Now when the sun was going down, a deep sleep fell upon Abram; and behold, horror and great darkness fell upon him. Then He said to Abram: Know certainly that your descendants will be strangers in a land that is not theirs, and will serve them, and they will afflict them four hundred years. And also the nation whom they serve I will judge; afterward they shall come out with great possessions. Now as for you, you shall go to your fathers in peace; you shall be buried at a good old age. But in the fourth generation they shall return here, for the iniquity of the Amorites is not yet complete." And it came to pass, when the sun went down and it was dark, that behold, there appeared a smoking oven and a burning torch that passed between those pieces. On the same day the Lord made a covenant with Abram, saying: "To your descendants I have given this land, from the river of Egypt to the great river, the River Euphrates—the Kenites, the Kenezzites, the Kadmonites, the Hittites, the Perizzites, the Rephaim, the Amorites, the Canaanites, the Girgashites, and the Jebusites."

In this covenant, we find many parallels with the New Covenant. We know that we can only enter into the New Covenant by faith. Abraham also had to believe in order to be part of the covenant that God made with him. As we see in verses five and six above, Abraham was required to believe:

Then He brought him outside and said, "Look now toward heaven, and count the stars if you are able to number them." And He said to him, "So shall your descendants be." *And he believed in the LORD, and He accounted it to him for righteousness.* (Emphasis mine)

As we see here, as well as in many other New Testament verses, faith was the requirement to be part of this covenant. Abraham had to believe first; then God made the covenant with him, and he could enter into it. The order is very clear, just as it is with the New Covenant. It is impossible for you to enter into the New Covenant by any other way than by faith in the finished work of the cross.

The Power of a Blood Covenant

A blood covenant was not an unusual thing between ancient Hebrew people. Even today, there are people groups, especially tribes in Africa, who still enter into blood covenants. It was considered the most powerful of all covenants, and once it was made, it was totally sacred. This covenant could by no means be broken by either of the two parties. Usually, when a blood covenant was made and one party broke it, their own family members would kill them for not keeping the blood covenant sacred.

The New Covenant that God made is a blood covenant as we will see later. Jesus took the wine, which was symbolic for His blood, and said; "This is the cup of My New Covenant." The very first sign in the Bible of blood flowing occurs in Genesis 3:21: "Also for Adam and his wife the

LORD God made tunics of skin, and clothed them." Where did God get the animal skin if not from an animal that He had killed? Adam and Eve did not need clothing just because they were cold or naked; this act expressed the desire of God to be in a blood covenant with man through Jesus Christ.

Once two parties enter into a blood covenant, it means that they are now perfectly united. There is no more separation or distinction between these two parties. Through the New Covenant, we have been perfectly united with Christ, and God makes no more distinction between His Son and us. This is why He is called the Head, and we are called the body—because those two things are inseparable. When Saul persecuted the Church, Jesus said that Saul was persecuting Him. This was an expression of the blood covenant of God with the Church.

The blood covenant also means that the stronger one has to protect the weaker one even if it costs him his life. What a beautiful sign of the New Covenant! Jesus was willing to lay down His life for us in order to keep us safe. The Bible says in Colossians 3:3 that we are "hidden with Christ in God." We are totally protected by the stronger

One, who is obviously God. Did Jesus not say that nobody could take us out of His hands? He, the stronger One, is holding us, the weaker ones, because of the blood covenant. I recently said to a pastor friend of mine that one of my friends gave his life to the Lord, to which he immediately replied, "That's good, but isn't it much better that the Lord gave His life to him?"

Another thing that a blood covenant involves is a sharing of each other's possessions. Neither of the two parties can claim anything as their own after making the covenant; there are no more divisions of properties. If one brought a million dollar debt into the covenant and the other brought ten million dollars in cash, there would then be no more debt for the first and nine million remaining dollars for the both of them together. The person who brought the debt into the covenant does not have to ask for anything; it simply belongs to him now. This is an important fact for you to remember and meditate about. I will show you later in this book that we Christians ask for too many things that already belong to us.

The Abrahamic Covenant and the Crucifixion

Remember that the New Covenant was sealed with the blood of Jesus. We will now discover some wonderful parallels between God's covenant with Abraham and the crucifixion. The first one is that God demanded a sacrifice. Genesis 15:9 tells us,

> So He said to him, "Bring Me a three-year-old heifer, a three-year-old female goat, a three-year-old ram, a turtledove, and a young pigeon." Then he brought all these to Him and cut them in two, down the middle, and placed each piece opposite the other; but he did not cut the birds in two.

When God came to Abraham to initiate the blood covenant, He demanded a sacrifice from Abraham. Those animals had to be cut into pieces, and blood had to flow. God also demanded a sacrifice from Jesus Christ so that the New Covenant could be made. The sacrifice that God demanded was the body of Jesus Christ Himself, which was also cut and torn in pieces and His blood shed. Hebrews 10:12 speaks of Jesus in this way: "But this man, after He had offered one sacrifice for sins forever, sat down at the right hand of God."

The second similarity we see between the story of Abraham and the crucifixion is that Abraham, as well as Christ on the cross, had to face darkness and great horrors. Look at Genesis 15:12 and Matthew 27:45:

> Now when the sun was going down, a deep sleep fell upon Abram; and behold, horror and great darkness fell upon him.
>
> —GENESIS 15:12

> Now from the sixth hour until the ninth hour there was darkness over all the land.
>
> —MATTHEW 27:45

As we see in the verse from Matthew, great darkness came all over the land; we also know that Christ had to face great horror during the crucifixion. Since Jesus became sin for us, He had to face all the horrors of sin.

The third parallel we see is that Abraham had to face the vultures. Genesis 15:11 tells us, "And when the vultures came down on the carcasses, Abram drove them away." It is important to notice that God, who was entering into a covenant with Abraham, did not help Abraham to drive the vultures away. In the typology of the Bible, vultures stand for demons. When Jesus was on the cross, He was left alone and had to face all the horrible demonic activity by Himself. Matthew 27:46 describes the horror that Jesus had to face alone:

> And about the ninth hour Jesus cried out with a loud voice, saying, "Eli, Eli, lama sabachthani?" that is, "My God, My God, why have You forsaken Me?"

As He cried out in agony and asked God why He was forsaken, heaven was silent. There was no response from God; He had to face His darkness alone just as Abraham did.

Chapter 11

The Mystery Revealed

As I said before, the New Covenant is the mystery that has been hidden in God as seen in the following two scriptures:

> Now to Him who is able to establish you according to my gospel and the preaching of Jesus Christ, according to the revelation of the mystery kept secret since the world began
>
> —ROMANS 16:25

> But we speak the wisdom of God in a mystery, the hidden wisdom which God ordained before the ages for our glory . . .
>
> —1 CORINTHIANS 2:7

Anything that has been hidden can either be revealed by the one who hid it or sometimes discovered by others through diligent searching. In these two scriptures, we can see that it (the New Covenant) had been hidden in God and kept secret since the world began. The word *mystery* in the original Greek means a hidden or secret thing, not obvious to the understanding.[1] Since the New Covenant is a mystery, which obviously means that it is not very plain to see or understand, it must be found or unraveled by clues given to us. It is like a hidden treasure that people diligently search for. This is one of the reasons why the Bible is such a fascinating book.

Here, in this blood covenant with Abraham (who, after all, is our father in the faith), we find the clues to this outstanding mystery. Let us go back to Genesis 15:17–18 to find some hints and start to unravel the mystery:

> And it came to pass, when the sun went down and it was dark, that behold, there appeared a smoking oven and a burning torch that passed between those pieces. On the same day the LORD made a covenant with Abram . . .

In order for us to see the clues here, we need to understand what the normal procedure of a blood covenant was. The two parties involved would take the animals that were to be sacrificed and cut them into two pieces, which then needed to be placed opposite each other. This was done by Abraham, which we clearly see in verses nine and ten:

So He said to him, "Bring Me a three-year-old heifer, a three-year-old female goat, a three-year-old ram, a turtledove, and a young pigeon." Then he brought all these to Him and cut them in two, down the middle, and placed each piece opposite the other; but he did not cut the birds in two.

It is important to notice that God never said anything about cutting the animals in two. He simply told Abraham to bring them to Him. Why did Abraham cut the animals in two without God instructing him to do that? I believe he did so because he understood how blood covenants were executed in his culture at that time.

What normally happened was that both parties had to walk between the cut pieces of the animals and say something like the following: "May it be done unto me as it was done to these animals should I ever break the covenant with you." Then the other party had to follow the same process. Sometimes they would both drink the animal's blood mingled with their own blood and sometimes they would even cut themselves on their wrists and mix their blood. Both parties always had to walk through the cut animals in order for the covenant to be ratified (or confirmed).

This part always brings tears to my eyes and joy to my heart. When God made the covenant with Abraham, He decided to put Abraham to sleep as we see in verses 12 and 17:

> Now when the sun was going down, a deep sleep fell upon Abram; and behold, horror and great darkness fell upon him. . . . And it came to pass, when the sun went down and it was dark, that behold, there appeared *a smoking oven and a burning torch* that passed between those pieces. (Emphasis mine)

How could God make a covenant with Abraham when Abraham never walked through the pieces of the animals? It is an amazing mystery. We are told that a deep sleep fell upon Abraham. Instead of Abraham and God walking through the cut pieces and ratifying the covenant, two other symbols walked through—a smoking oven and a burning torch.

Who did the two symbols represent? Obviously, one must have been God, as it was He who initiated and made the covenant with Abraham. Here we see one of the first, most powerful clues to the New Covenant in the Bible. Since God represented the smoking oven, it was Jesus who represented the burning torch. This is what makes the New Covenant so secure. It was ratified between God the Father and His Son Jesus Christ. When Abraham awoke from his sleep, the only thing he had to do was to enter into this covenant by simple faith. Here is the first time we see a prophetic picture of the most powerful words in the Bible from John 19:30: "It is finished!" After they finished the ratification of the blood covenant, God the Father and His Son Jesus woke up Abraham and presented it to him.

We know that the Bible says that we were dead in our trespasses and sin (Eph. 2:1). Of course, before we got saved, we were not literally dead, but we were spiritually dead—as in a deep, spiritual sleep. While we were in that state, God the Father and Jesus His Son made a perfect blood covenant with each other, woke us up from our spiritual sleep, and presented it to us. We only had to enter it by simple faith alone. It is truly finished!

I am sure you would like to know how I concluded that it was God and Jesus who walked through the animal pieces in the story above. Since it is a mystery, we have to continue to unravel the clues. Remember that the two pieces that walked through were a smoking oven and a burning torch. God the Father represents the smoking oven, which Bible scholars agree on. First, because God who made the covenant had no choice but to walk through it—and second, Exodus 13:21 tells us,

> And the Lord went before them by day in a pillar of cloud to lead the way, and by night in a *pillar of fire* to give them light, so as to go by day and night. (Emphasis mine)

In the original, the expression used here for "pillar of fire" means a smoking fire. One of the original meanings for *oven* is a firepot.[2] Do you see the clue? God, who walked with His people as a smoking fire, walked through the pieces as the smoking oven (firepot). Needless to say, at that time, they did not have electric ovens, but used ovens that had an open fire which caused smoke.

Jesus represented the flaming torch, which we can easily see from clues that He Himself gave to us. In John 1:9, we are told, "That was the true Light which gives light to every man coming into the world." Out of the mouth of Jesus Himself, come these words in John 8:12:

> Then Jesus spoke to them again, saying, "I am the light of the world. He who follows Me shall not walk in darkness, but have the light of life."

In both scriptures, we are told that it is Jesus that is the light. If you look into the original Greek, from which our Bibles are translated, you will find that the meaning for *light* is "torch."[3] The picture is getting clearer, and the puzzle pieces are starting to fit together. The Father and Jesus made an eternal covenant and included Abraham in it without any of his own doing.

Further Clues to the Mystery

In the following chapters, you will see the importance of the fact that Jesus and the Father made this eternal covenant with each other. I would like to show you some more fascinating clues that unravel this mystery we call the New Covenant. In John 8:56–59, Jesus is in a confrontation with the Jews:

"Your father Abraham rejoiced to see My day, and he saw it and was glad." Then the Jews said to Him, "You are not yet fifty years old, and have You seen Abraham?" Jesus said to them, "Most assuredly, I say to you, before Abraham was, I AM." Then they took up stones to throw at Him; but Jesus hid Himself and went out of the temple, going through the midst of them, and so passed by.

—JOHN 8:56–59

Jesus said something that made the Jews so angry that they took up stones to throw at Him in order to kill Him. What was it that made them so angry? Jesus told them that Abraham saw His own day and rejoiced. This was the first thing that upset them because He was still young, and in their opinion, could not have been around during the time of Abraham. How could Jesus say that Abraham saw His day? Jesus was never mentioned in the life of Abraham. The Jews told Him, "You are not even fifty years old; how can You say that You have seen Abraham?" It is very interesting to notice that the Jews twisted the statement of Jesus. Jesus never said that He saw Abraham, but rather that Abraham saw His day.

Yet the Jews asked Him, "How could You have seen Abraham?"

When Jesus said that Abraham rejoiced to see His day, He was referring to the event of the ratification of the blood covenant in Genesis 15. How could Abraham know about Jesus since the Bible never mentions Jesus in the life of Abraham? Since it is a mystery, there can be no direct mention, but only clues that lead us to the uncovering of this secret. Galatians 3:8 tells us,

> And the Scripture, foreseeing that God would justify the Gentiles by faith, *preached the gospel to Abraham* beforehand, saying, "In you all the nations shall be blessed." (Emphasis mine)

Here we are told that God preached the gospel to Abraham. The gospel is the good news of the New Covenant. When did God ever preach the gospel to Abraham and talk to him about the New Covenant? After God made the Covenant in Genesis 15, He said in Genesis 18:18 that all the nations of the earth would be blessed in Abraham. We do understand that all the nations of the world have not entered into the New Covenant by following Abraham, but rather by following Christ. Since the Abrahamic Covenant was made between God and Jesus, the two parties that walked through the pieces, the New Covenant has been made between God and Jesus. Let us look at one last scripture in order to see that Jesus was the other partner in this Covenant. Galatians 3:16 tells us,

> Now to Abraham and his Seed were the promises made. He does not say, "And to seeds," as of many, but as of one, *"And to your Seed," who is Christ.* (Emphasis mine)

Let me summarize what we have seen: God preached the gospel, the good news of the New Covenant, to Abraham. When the covenant between God and Abraham was made, Abraham was sound asleep, yet there could be no blood covenant unless two parties walked through the cut pieces of the animals. God, who made the covenant with His Son Jesus and included Abraham through faith alone, also had to make the promises to the other partner in the covenant. Since the other partner in the covenant was Jesus and not Abraham, God had to make the promises to Christ. We just saw in Galatians 3:16 that the Bible says, "That to Abraham and his seed (singular) the promises were made." Then Paul says, "That seed is Christ." The Father made His covenant with His Son Jesus Christ and made His promises to Him, as we have just seen in Galatians 3:16.

In the next chapter, I will show you further biblical proof of this wonderful mystery. We must understand that the New Covenant and the Abrahamic Covenant run on the same line. Both of them depend on God and His Son Jesus Christ. And as Abraham only entered into the covenant by faith in what Jesus did, so we also, as the children of Abraham, can only enter into the New Covenant by faith.

The important thing to understand is that we must believe, not just in Jesus our Savior, but also in the One who sealed the New Covenant and offered it to us to enter in by faith. If you limit your faith to believing for forgiveness of sin and going to heaven, that is all you will get. If you, however, enter by faith into this amazingly superb New Covenant, you will get all its benefits. Remember, our works can never earn the benefits of this incredible New Covenant. If they could, it would mean that the New Covenant runs on the same line as the Old Covenant. Since it runs on the same line as the covenant with Abraham, its benefits can only be received in the same way as Abraham received them, which is by faith alone.

Endnotes

1. *mustérion,* "a mystery or secret doctrine"; Strong's #3466; http://biblehub.com/greek/3466.htm; accessed 19 June 2017.

2. *tannur,* "stove, firepot": Strong's #8574; http://biblehub.com/hebrew/8574.htm; accessed 19 June 2017.

3. *phós,* "light"; Strong's #5457; http://biblehub.com/greek/5457.htm; accessed 19 June 2017.

Chapter 12

Understanding the New Covenant

We cannot live in all the benefits of the New Covenant experientially unless we truly understand it. Every Christian probably believes in the New Covenant. However, what they believe about it and how they apply it in their lives differs greatly. The important point is not whether there is a New Covenant or not, but how was it made and how we can fully enter into it? As we have seen in the previous chapter, the Abrahamic Covenant begins to reveal the mystery of the New Covenant, and it was made between God the Father and His Son, Jesus Christ; Abraham was invited into it by faith.

As we read through the epistles of the New Testament, especially the epistles of Paul, it seems so clear that there is no other plan for the people of God except a life of absolute victory. My mind goes to statements like "All things work together for good; we are more than conquerors; we can do all things through Christ who strengthens us; God always leads us into victory," and similar statements. Why is the experience of the majority of Christians not this kind of victorious life? Why do Christians all over the world live a life of defeat, struggle against sinful habits, and live a life of ups and downs? The answer is that they do not fully understand, believe, or walk in the New Covenant. Only through the New Covenant will our full potential be released.

I will still show you in this book how much Old Covenant thinking and practice is mixed into the life of the average Christian. As I demonstrate these wrong beliefs and practices to you, I am sure you will find that you are involved in some of them. Very subtly our minds have been infiltrated with a mixture of Old Covenant beliefs and New Covenant mindsets. The danger lies in the subtleness and in the mixture of these two very different mindsets.

It is common knowledge that music powerfully influences our minds and hearts. We all know those songs that get stuck in our heads; we have a hard time getting them out. Most Christians are not aware that week after week they sing songs in church services with messages from both the Old and the New Covenants. I believe that the writers of these songs meant very well when they wrote them. They simply did not have clear revelation of the New Covenant.

I have been very aware of this mixture of Old Covenant phrases into Christian songs for a long time now. I will not sing any songs that have Old Covenant principles in them. Many of these songs are wonderful songs filled with New Covenant truth, and then suddenly there is a line which is clearly from the Old Covenant mixed into it.

I was recently one of the preachers at a conference together with another well-known pastor. Just before he had to preach, the worship team sang a song with a beautiful tune that talked about the river that flows from the throne of God. It was a wonderful song with great words until it came to the last line, which said repeatedly, "Wash me; wash me." I turned to the pastor next to me, who was about to preach, and asked him, "Are you dirty? Because I am not. I have been washed and cleansed by the blood of Jesus Christ. I have been made perfectly pure and righteous through the New Covenant." By the way, that pastor had also not sung the song.

A good friend and pastor said to me just a few weeks ago that when he first heard me talk about these things he thought that I was just extreme, critical, and picky. But as he began to study the Scriptures and began to look at his own life in the light of the New Covenant, he realized how much he was missing out on and how important these things truly are. I certainly do not want to be critical, but I do not want to be destroyed by ignorance. Vladimir Lenin, who is considered the father of Communism, said that if a lie is told often enough, it becomes a truth. If we keep singing Old Covenant statements week after week, in our hearts they will become the truth, and it will be very difficult to walk in the blessings and benefits of the New Covenant. This is why I am very careful what I sing.

I will continue to unveil this wonderful mystery of the New Covenant, which is so radical and yet so amazing that it is often hard to truly grasp. The reason for this is that the church as a whole, for about seventeen hundred years has not walked purely in the New Covenant. It is my own conviction that grasping the New Covenant with our whole heart has the potential to change every single area of our life and turn it into a life of total victory. Is it not the true and deep heart's desire of every Christian to live a life pleasing to God? Do we not all one day want to hear our Master say these wonderful words to us, "Well done, you good and faithful servant"? This can only be achieved by entering into and living fully in the New Covenant.

With Whom Did God Make the New Covenant?

The answer to this question seems very simple; most Christians would say that God made the New Covenant with us. I do not believe this is the correct answer, and I will give you clear biblical arguments to prove it. We have already seen from the covenant with Abraham that the covenant was made between God and Jesus and that Abraham entered into it by faith. I know that Genesis 15 tells us that on that day God made a covenant with Abraham, but the fact that Abraham never walked through the parts of the sacrifice means God made it indirectly, not directly, with him. The covenant was made directly between God the Father and Jesus Christ. It is of utmost importance that we understand this truth since so much depends on it.

The New Covenant has, therefore, been made directly between God and Jesus. This is the reason why it is so secure—because it does not depend on us. Any covenant that has been made between two parties obviously depends on the two parties between whom it was made. Therefore, if the New Covenant had been made between you or the Church and God, it would again depend on you or the Church to keep our respective part.

Look at your own life and answer a simple question honestly. Have you ever sinned or failed since you have become a Christian? The obvious answer is "Yes." If the New Covenant had been between you and God, what would have happened when you sinned? Would it have affected the covenant between God and you? Of course, it would have. Remember that a covenant means a bond between two parties and defines the way they relate to each other. Christians live under guilt, condemnation, and defeat because they still believe that the way God relates to them depends on them.

Biblical Arguments

Here are a number of biblical arguments, which show you that the New Covenant is not between you and God, but, more accurately, between God and Jesus. First, there is not a single promise in the entire Bible that I could find where a direct covenant has been promised or made between God and the Gentiles. We Christians, who are not Jews by nature, were Gentiles before we got saved. This may sound very confusing since a covenant is a bond between two parties and the Bible talks a lot about the New Covenant. Furthermore, I have built the chapters in this book so far to show you the wonderful New Covenant that belongs to us. Now I say that there is no such bond or covenant between God and us. Let me clarify. Of course, there is a New Covenant, and it is the most amazing truth of the entire Bible. The important aspect is that it has not been made directly between God and us. It has been made between God and Jesus Christ, and we enter into it by faith alone.

Remember the scripture from Jeremiah 31 where God announced the New Covenant and the three new things that were a part of it? I would like to remind you that it said, "This is the covenant that I will make with the house of Israel and the house of Judah." God is addressing Israel through the prophet Jeremiah—and not the Gentiles. This fact caused so much confusion and problems in the early church. The Jews refused to accept that there is a covenant between the Gentiles and God. As we saw before, God had to go out of His way to convince Peter that there is a New Covenant that involves the Gentiles.

This fact is so hard to grasp for many Christians because it is a mystery and not written in plain language in the Scriptures. When I discovered this mystery, my heart burst with joy. Suddenly, I understood that my covenant with God was perfectly secure because it did not depend on me but on God the Father and His Son Jesus Christ. Neither of those two will ever break this covenant because they are both faithful in nature. Therefore, no matter what I do, it will not affect this covenant relationship.

Let me repeat again, a covenant is a bond between two people defining how they relate to each other. My failure will not alter the way God relates to me since by legal bond He can only relate to me according to who I am in Christ Jesus. He will always treat me the same way that He treats Jesus, His beloved Son.

Since the New Covenant is neither a continuation nor a renewing of the Old Covenant, which was totally removed in Christ, but runs on the same line as the Abrahamic Covenant, we must look at what the Bible says about our (the Gentile believer's) relationship with Abraham. Carefully look at the following scriptures:

Therefore know that only those who are of faith are sons of Abraham.

—GALATIANS 3:7

And the Scripture, foreseeing that God would justify the Gentiles by faith, preached the gospel to Abraham beforehand, saying, "In you all the nations shall be blessed."

—GALATIANS 3:8

So then those who are of faith are blessed with believing Abraham.

—GALATIANS 3:9

. . . that the blessing of Abraham might come upon the Gentiles in Christ Jesus, that we might receive the promise of the Spirit through faith.

—GALATIANS 3:14

Now to Abraham and his Seed were the promises made. He does not say, "And to seeds," as of many, but as of one, "And to your Seed," who is Christ.

—GALATIANS 3:16

> And if you are Christ's, then you are Abraham's seed, and heirs according to the promise.
>
> —GALATIANS 3:29

In these scriptures, we can see that we entered into the New Covenant blessing in the same way that Abraham did—by faith alone. The scriptures from the letter to the Galatians connect Gentile believers directly to the covenant of Abraham. Let us look at these important verses from the letter to the Hebrews:

> For when God made a promise to Abraham, because He could swear by no one greater, He swore by Himself, saying, "Surely blessing I will bless you, and multiplying I will multiply you." And so, after he had patiently endured, he obtained the promise. For men indeed swear by the greater, and an oath for confirmation is for them an end of all dispute. Thus God, determining to show more abundantly to the heirs of promise the immutability of His counsel, confirmed it by an oath, that by two immutable things, in

which it is impossible for God to lie, we might have strong consolation, who have fled for refuge to lay hold of the hope set before us. This hope we have as an anchor of the soul, both sure and steadfast, and which enters the Presence behind the veil, where the forerunner has entered for us, even Jesus, having become High Priest forever according to the order of Melchizedek.

—HEBREWS 6:13–20

These verses clearly explain that the New Covenant is directly connected to the Abrahamic Covenant. The writer starts out in verse thirteen just talking about Abraham and his covenant, showing that God made it by swearing by Himself. In verse seventeen, he brings Gentiles into it by calling us heirs of promise, which, as we have seen from the verses in Galatians, refers to us. Verses nineteen and twenty suddenly switch from the Abrahamic Covenant to the New Covenant without any explanation. He is telling us that our Covenant is so sure and steadfast because Jesus Himself entered into the Most Holy Place as our great High Priest. He did so in order to seal the New Covenant.

Chapter 13

The Covenant between the Father and the Son

I will give you further proof in this chapter that the New Covenant was made between God the Father and His Son Jesus Christ. The first evidence of this Covenant is that not a single New Testament writer speaks about Christians being directly brought into a new covenant with God. When God made a covenant with the people of Israel, they knew exactly what was happening. There was a ceremony, the sprinkling of blood; the terms were clearly outlined to them, and they responded affirmatively to that covenant.

Nowhere in the New Testament do we see such a ceremony or act connected with the New Covenant. The very first time in the New Testament that the New Covenant is even mentioned is when Jesus announced it at the Last Supper just before His crucifixion. That night there was no ceremony, no shedding of blood, and no response required from the disciples. It was simply an announcement of what was about to happen. If God had made a New Covenant directly with us Christians, as with every covenant, there would have been a ceremony or an act and a response. Somewhere, some Christian would have had to be part of this, representing all the Christians that are part of this New Covenant. But that never happened; therefore, I believe that God never made a New Covenant directly with us. Instead, He made it with His Son Jesus, and we are included in it by faith.

This might seem insignificant to you, but it is very important because the covenant defines how God relates to us and how we relate to Him. Since it was made with Jesus and we are included by faith, all we have to do is believe that we are "in Christ" and every single benefit of the covenant belongs to us. I will explain this in more detail later. The next clear evidence is found in Revelation 11:19:

> Then the temple of God was opened in heaven, and the ark of His covenant was seen in His temple. And there were lightnings, noises, thunderings, an earthquake, and great hail.

Here we see that the Ark of the Covenant is now in heaven. If the New Covenant had been directly between God and us the Church, then God would have to give us an Ark of this New Covenant. But since the covenant was between God and Jesus, the Ark of the Covenant is now in heaven. Hebrews 9:11–12 clearly describes the ceremony in heaven:

> But Christ came as High Priest of the good things to come, with the greater and more perfect tabernacle not made with hands, that is, not of this creation. Not with the blood of goats and calves, but with His own blood He entered the Most Holy Place once for all, having obtained eternal redemption.

These verses speak of the ratifying of the New Covenant which Jesus Christ our High Priest did. It tells us about the more perfect tabernacle that was not made with hands and is not of this creation. Jesus Himself, after His death on the cross, entered heaven with His own perfect blood and sealed the New Covenant between God and Himself.

The third evidence is found in the high priestly prayer in John 17:10: "And all Mine are Yours, and Yours are Mine, and I am glorified in them." We must remember that Jesus lived in a Hebrew culture that understood covenants. The way Jesus addressed His Father was not like a normal father and son conversation. In Hebrew culture, a son did not own everything that the father had; he could only claim his legal inheritance. Jesus said here that everything that belonged to God belonged to Him, which is very clear covenant language. Once two people entered into a covenant, there were no more dividing lines about what belonged to whom. Since the New Covenant was before the foundation of the world, Christ could say to His Father that everything of His was God's and everything of God's was His.

Maybe you say, well, Jesus was God; therefore, of course everything that belonged to His Father belonged to Him too. Hang on a minute, my dear friend. Jesus prayed this prayer as He lived on earth; He did not access His Godhead, but lived as a man. Look at this scripture in Philippians 2:7:

> . . . but made Himself of no
> reputation, taking the form of a

bondservant, and coming in the likeness of men.

The word for *reputation* in the original Greek has an interesting meaning, which is to make empty.[1] Since Jesus emptied Himself of all the equality with God, all that belonged to the Father did not belong to Him simply because He was God. It belonged to Him because they entered into an eternal covenant from the foundation of the world, just out of love for you and me.

The Prophet Isaiah

The different Old Testament prophets had glimpses of the New Covenant. We saw earlier that on the road to Emmaus Jesus taught about Himself and the New Covenant using Moses and the Prophets. The clearest revelation about this subject that any of the prophets had was given to Isaiah. Most Christians are familiar with and treasure Isaiah 53. Countless people have, like the Ethiopian eunuch in Acts 8, found Christ through this passage and entered into the New Covenant. Millions of people have risen from their sickbeds or deathbeds by claiming verse five of that chapter which says, "But He was wounded for our transgressions, He was bruised for our iniquities;

the chastisement for our peace was upon Him, and by His stripes we are healed."

Unfortunately, many passages in the Bible are misunderstood simply because of the division of chapters and verses. These were not put there by the original writers or by God, but by the men who translated the manuscripts. They did so in order to create reference points so we might find things more easily. Often they made divisions in places where they should not have been made. We must look at everything in Scripture in its proper context, according to one of the major rules of Bible interpretation.

It is very clear and beyond argument that chapter 53 of Isaiah speaks about the death and crucifixion of Jesus. It paints a very graphic and detailed picture of what would and then did happen on the cross. It is also beyond argument that through what happened on the cross, we have received the New Covenant. In the context of this prophetic revelation of the crucifixion, the New Covenant is also mentioned. Let us look at Isaiah 54:9–10, which talks about two Covenants—the Covenant of Noah and the New Covenant:

"For this is like the waters of Noah to Me; for as I have sworn that the waters of Noah would no longer cover the earth, *so have I sworn that I would not be angry with you, nor rebuke you.* For the mountains shall depart and the hills be removed, but My kindness shall not depart from you, *nor shall My covenant of peace be removed,"* says the LORD, who has mercy on you. (Emphasis mine)

God is saying that never, in all eternity, will this covenant of peace be removed. Who was God angry with in Isaiah 53? The answer, of course, is with His Son Jesus. Because Jesus became sin for us on the cross, He had to face God's wrath for us. Here we see beautiful covenant language when God says, "I have *sworn* that I would not be angry with you" (Emphasis mine).

"For a mere moment I have forsaken you, but with great mercies I will gather you. With a little wrath I hid My face from you for a moment; but with everlasting kindness I will have mercy on you," says the LORD, your Redeemer.

—ISAIAH 54:7–8

We are told that God hid His face for a moment. From whom did He hide His face in the context of this scripture? Since this chapter talks about the crucifixion, it is clear that He hid His face from Jesus. God also told Jesus that after this brief moment of suffering and rejection, there would be an eternal covenant between the two of them, which means that the New Covenant is between God and Jesus. I will soon show you in one of the following chapters that this is of absolute importance for your life of victory.

We are given a graphic description—not only of the suffering of Jesus, but also of the anger of God He experienced. Verse ten tells us that it pleased the Lord to bruise Him; God put Jesus through anguish. In this context, God tells Him that He has sworn that He will never be angry with Him again or rebuke Him because of His covenant of peace. As we connect this passage to Hebrews 7:21–22, we see that God uses one of the same words that He used in Isaiah 54:9:

> . . . (for they have become priests
> without an oath, but He with an oath
> by Him who said to Him: "The Lord
> has *sworn* and will not relent, 'You are

a priest forever according to the order of Melchizedek'"); by so much more Jesus has become a surety of a better covenant. (Emphasis mine)

Here God says that He *swore* that Jesus is the eternal priest and the guarantee of the better covenant, which is our New Covenant. In Isaiah 54, God also *swore* that there would be no more anger and that the covenant of peace would last forever. We see in these two chapters of Isaiah that the covenant was made between God and His Son. We see both parties entering into an eternal covenant in order to redeem mankind. The terms of the covenant are clearly outlined. The Son would pay the price of suffering, laying down His life for us, and the Father would accept the sacrifice. His wrath would be appeased, and God would give Jesus the reward, which is the salvation of humanity and a beautiful bride, His Church. Look at the following verses from Isaiah 53, and you will see the New Covenant between God and Jesus:

He is despised and rejected by men, a Man of sorrows and acquainted with grief. And we hid, as it were, our faces from Him; He was despised, and we did not esteem Him. Surely

He has borne our griefs and carried our sorrows; yet we esteemed Him stricken, smitten by God, and afflicted. But He was wounded for our transgressions, He was bruised for our iniquities; the chastisement for our peace was upon Him, and by His stripes we are healed.

—ISAIAH 53:3–5

He shall see the labor of His soul, and be satisfied. By His knowledge My righteous Servant shall justify many, for He shall bear their iniquities. Therefore I will divide Him a portion with the great, and He shall divide the spoil with the strong, because He poured out His soul unto death, and He was numbered with the transgressors, and He bore the sin of many, and made intercession for the transgressors.

—ISAIAH 53:11–12

Jesus was never killed at the cross; He willingly laid down His life and so entered into this Covenant with His Father. It was the plan of an amazingly loving God, which was hidden from the ages and has been revealed by the Holy Spirit.

Please do not limit the death of Jesus on the cross
to only the forgiveness of sin and the healing of
your body. Always remember, it is the sealing of an
eternal covenant between God and Jesus Christ.

One Final Argument

The argument remains that the prophet Jeremiah
says that the New Covenant is between God and
Israel. The New Testament writers understood that
Jesus was the new Israel. I will show you three
verses that will prove to you that in the New
Testament Israel is symbolic for Jesus. The first
passage occurs in Exodus 4:

> Then you shall say to Pharaoh,
> "Thus says the Lord: 'Israel is my
> son, My firstborn. So I say to you, let
> My son go that he may serve Me.'"
> —EXODUS 4:22–23

If I were to ask you who is God calling His
son here, you would without doubt say, "Israel."
The answer is correct. God called Israel out of
Egypt and told Pharaoh he had to let them go. He
called Israel His son. Let us look at the second
verse from the prophet Hosea 11:1: "When Israel
was a child, I loved him, and out of Egypt I

called My son."

Now let us make the same test again. I will ask you, "Who is God talking about here through the mouth of the prophet Hosea?" No doubt your answer again would be, "Israel." This time I would say to you, "Are you sure that God is talking about Israel?" It sounds like an exact quotation of what happened in Exodus 4:22–23 where He was talking about Israel. God called Israel His child and son and called him out of Egypt. Let us connect it with a third scripture in Matthew 2:14–15:

> When he arose, he took the young Child and his mother by night and departed for Egypt, and was there until the death of Herod that it might be fulfilled which was spoken by the Lord through the prophet saying, "Out of Egypt I called My son."

What does Matthew mean by quoting Hosea and saying that Jesus fulfilled this passage? He clearly says, "Out of Egypt I called My Son," but Hosea adds that Israel was the son. Here we see the pieces fitting again, and the mystery being revealed.

Jesus was understood to be Israel. This is my final argument that the New Covenant, which Jeremiah said is between Israel and God, is between Jesus and God since Jesus represents Israel.

Endnote

1. *kenoó*, "to empty"; Strong's #2758; http://biblehub.com/greek/2758.htm; accessed 19 June 2017.

Chapter 14

What about Us?

Now that the picture of this amazing New Covenant is becoming clearer, we must ask this important question: how does all this apply to us and work out in our daily lives? Throughout the next few chapters, I will not only answer these questions, but I will make it as practical as possible so that you might walk experientially in this wonderful truth of the New Covenant. First, let us look at one more important aspect.

The Announcement of Jesus

If we truly understood what happened at the Last Supper and the importance of this wonderful sacrament, I believe we would celebrate it more often. In Matthew 26:17–19, we read about the last moments in the life of Jesus when He was together with His disciples:

> Now on the first day of the Feast of the Unleavened Bread the disciples came to Jesus, saying to Him,

"Where do You want us to prepare for You to eat the Passover?" And He said, "Go into the city to a certain man, and say to him, 'The Teacher says, "My time is at hand; I will keep the Passover at your house with My disciples."'" So the disciples did as Jesus had directed them; and they prepared the Passover.

Jesus was celebrating the Passover, which is a Jewish festival in remembrance of their deliverance out of Egypt. I am sure you are familiar with the story of the ten plagues, which God brought upon the Egyptians. After Pharaoh stubbornly refused to let the Israelites go, God did a final thing, which was a shadow of the New Covenant. An innocent lamb had to be killed; the blood had to be applied to the doorposts; and the meat had to be eaten. That night, the angel of the Lord walked through Egypt and killed every firstborn son in every house that did not have the blood on its doorposts. What a great victory for the people of Israel who were finally allowed to leave the slavery of Egypt!

The Jews celebrated the Passover once a year in order to remember that night of deliverance. It was a common practice that Jesus also did with His disciples. It was that time of year again when the disciples asked Jesus, "Where do You want us to celebrate the Passover?" In the middle of this ceremony, while they were eating and celebrating a victory of the past, Jesus did something prophetic that the disciples did not understand at the time. He announced the glorious New Covenant, which was about to come. Matthew 26:26–28 tells us this story:

> And as they were eating, Jesus took bread, blessed and broke it, and gave it to the disciples and said, "Take, eat; this is My body." Then He took the cup, and gave thanks, and gave it to them, saying, "Drink from it, all of you. *For this is My blood of the New Covenant,* which is shed for many for the remission of sins." (Emphasis mine)

This announcement was so radical and so new that they could not understand it. After Jesus told them to eat the bread, which was His body, He then took the cup and told all of them to drink from it because it was the blood of the New Covenant. Jesus Himself was smitten, beaten, cut open, and His blood shed so that the New Covenant between God and Him could be ratified.

I highly recommend that every believer in the New Covenant celebrate the Lord's Supper on a daily basis. If you are married, do it with your spouse. If you have family, do it with them. If you do not have either of those two possibilities, find some friends to do it together with. You can even celebrate it alone. But do not do it as a ritual or religious exercise; do it in full awareness of the amazing New Covenant that belongs to you now.

When I travel, I often carry crackers and a small bottle with me with some wine in it, and in the evening before going to bed, I celebrate the Lord's Supper on my own. I have had many wonderful experiences in doing this. I love to hold the cup of wine high toward heaven and thank Jesus for the blood of the New Covenant. Remember, Jesus said that on the night that He was betrayed the wine was His "blood of the new covenant."

Entering into This Covenant

I have already mentioned that we can only enter into the New Covenant by faith. How do we do that practically? Faith can be such an abstract thing, which many Christians struggle to live by. In the Christian world, however, it is the only currency that heaven accepts. Everything that Christ paid for on the cross can only become our experience by faith. Since we have a father of the faith, with whom God entered into a blood covenant, it is probably a good idea to learn our lessons of faith from him. Allow Abraham to teach you some valuable principles regarding the life of faith.

It is impossible to inherit the blessings of Abraham with the faith of Thomas. Abraham was willing to believe without seeing, while Thomas had the attitude that he would not believe until he saw (John 20:24–25). In order to learn these lessons from Abraham, we need to carefully read the passage when God made the covenant with him. Let us read Genesis 15:1–9 again:

> After these things the word of the LORD came to Abram in a vision, saying, "Do not be afraid, Abram. I am your shield, your exceedingly great reward." But Abram said, "Lord GOD, what will You give me, seeing I go childless, and the heir of my house is Eliezer of Damascus?" Then Abram said, ""Look, You have given me no offspring; indeed one born in my house is my heir!" And

behold, the word of the LORD came to him, saying, "This one shall not be your heir, but one who will come from your own body shall be your heir." Then He brought him outside and said, "Look now toward heaven, and count the stars if you are able to number them." And He said to him, "So shall your descendants be." And he believed in the LORD, and He accounted it to him for righteousness. Then He said to him, "I am the LORD, who brought you out of Ur of the Chaldeans, to give you this land to inherit it." And he said, "Lord GOD, how shall I know that I will inherit it?" So He said to him, "Bring Me a three-year-old heifer, a three-year-old female goat, a three-year-old ram, a turtledove, and a young pigeon."

The first thing we notice in this journey of Abraham's faith is that God Himself initiated it. Look carefully at verse one, please, where it says,

After these things the word of the Lord came to Abram in a vision, saying, :Do not be afraid, Abram. I am your shield, your exceedingly great reward."

Abraham did not come to God asking for anything. It was God who took the initiative, which is an important aspect of the New Covenant. We cannot enter the blessings of the New Covenant by our own efforts. Everything in the New Covenant has to start with John 19:30, where Jesus said, "It is finished!" We see a beautiful parallel between the Abrahamic Covenant and the New Covenant in this very first verse. Just as God initiated this covenant with Abraham, in the same way He initiated the New Covenant for us. It was in the heart of God since before the beginning of time. We are told in Colossians 1:26–27,

> . . . the mystery which has been hidden from ages and from generations, but now has been revealed to His saints. To them God willed to make known what are the riches of the glory of this mystery among the Gentiles: which is Christ in you, the hope of glory.

We see here that the New Covenant was in the heart of God from ages and generations. If you have an attitude that you have to initiate anything with God, you will not be able to experience the benefits of the New Covenant. Unfortunately, through our religious convictions, we have misinterpreted many scriptures.

Let us take Jeremiah 29:13, which says, "And you will seek Me and find Me, when you search for Me with all of your heart." This scripture has been preached by many well-meaning preachers and interpreted through an Old Covenant theology. They have presented God as someone who was hiding from people and made it sound like we have to initiate our pursuit of God in order to find Him. However, this is interpreted wrongly and taken out of context. In the context, God tells us that His thoughts toward us are thoughts of peace and not of evil, to give us a hope and a future. It is God who takes the initiative; we just need to respond to Him.

Please do not try to have faith in your faith or try to use faith to get something from God that you want. That is not how the New Covenant works. You would do much better taking time to truly understand the amazing heart of our loving God, who initiated the New Covenant out of pure love for you, just as He initiated the covenant with Abraham. The next thing we see in the life of faith of our father Abraham is that after God initiated that wonderful journey, Abraham told God his honest feelings, even questioning what God had just promised him. After God said that He Himself would be Abraham's shield and exceedingly great reward, Abraham questioned it by saying, "Lord, what will You give me, seeing that I go childless?" There is a big difference between an evil heart of unbelief (Heb. 3:12) and trying to understand what God is saying and doing in our lives. Abraham obviously did not have an evil heart of unbelief as we see from the context. He simply did not understand what God was doing in his life. God is a heart-God and relates to us that way— from His heart to our heart.

In the following story, we will understand why God was neither angry nor upset with Abraham when he questioned God. In Luke 1, we see two people with a similar experience, having a similar reaction, yet one was rebuked, and the other was blessed. Mary, the mother of Jesus, and

Zacharias, the father of John the Baptist, were both visited by the same angel, Gabriel. Both of them were told that they would have a child, and both of them reacted in astonishment. Their reactions look the same, yet the angel rebukes Zacharias and even disciplines him, while Gabriel kindly and patiently explains everything to Mary and blesses her. Look carefully at these verses:

> But the angel said to him, "Do not be afraid, Zacharias, for your prayer is heard; and your wife Elizabeth will bear you a son, and you shall call his name John."
>
> —LUKE 1:13

> And Zacharias said to the angel, "How shall I know this? For I am an old man, and my wife is well advanced in years."
>
> —LUKE 1:18

In these two verses, the angel tells him that they will have a child, and Zacharias wants to know how that could be. In the following verses, we see that because of that reaction, he was rebuked by Gabriel and was disciplined by being made mute.

> And the angel answered and said to him, "I am Gabriel, who stands in the presence of God, and was sent to speak to you and bring you these glad tidings. But behold, you will be mute and not able to speak until the day these things take place, because you did not believe my words which

will be fulfilled in their own time."

Now let us look at how Mary reacted to the angel and how Gabriel responded to her. Her reaction to the angel was almost word-for-word the same as Zacharias', yet Gabriel did not rebuke her. This reminds me of our story of Abraham who also questioned God, yet God did not rebuke him either. Why did God treat Mary and Zacharias so differently? The answer is very clear which we will see momentarily.

> Then the angel said to her, "Do not be afraid, Mary, for you have found favor with God." And behold, you will conceive in your womb and bring forth a Son, and shall call His name JESUS.
>
> —LUKE 1:30–31

> Then Mary said to the angel, "How can this be, since I do not know a man?" And the angel answered and said to her, "The Holy Spirit will come upon you, and the power of the Highest will overshadow you; therefore, also, that Holy One who is

to be born will be called the Son of God."

—Luke 1:34–35

The difference was in the heart attitude of these two people. Zacharias had a heart of unbelief while Mary simply wanted to understand what God was doing in her life. When Gabriel rebuked Zacharias, he specifically did so because of his unbelief as seen in verse 20:

> But behold, you will be mute and not able to speak until the day these things take place, because *you did not believe* my words which will be fulfilled in their own time. (Emphasis mine)

In verse 38, we see that Mary had a completely different heart attitude. She questioned Gabriel's words not out of unbelief, but out of a desire to understand the dealings of God with her:

> "Then Mary said, "Behold the maidservant of the Lord! *Let it be to me according to your word.*" (Emphasis mine)

It is very important in our walk of faith and the New Covenant to watch our heart attitude and reject any unbelief. God has no problem if you question Him in order to try to understand His ways with you. Unbelief, however, will rob you of every spiritual blessing.

Let us go back to Abraham's journey of faith. After God initiated the journey and Abraham questioned it, God took him outside and gave him another promise:

> Then He brought him outside and said, "Look now toward heaven, and count the stars if you are able to number them." And He said to him, "So shall your descendants be." And he believed in the LORD, and He accounted it to him for righteousness.
>
> —GENESIS 15:5–6

Here we have the first mention of the word *believe* in the entire Bible. Therefore, it is in this passage that we learn our lessons for the life of faith, which we need in order to experience the New Covenant. Let me show you, in this passage, five important things that took place:

1. God initiated it all.

2. Abraham questioned God—not
out of a heart of unbelief, but
simply in order to understand
the ways of God.
3. God gave him a clear promise.
4. Abraham made the choice to
believe God against all natural
circumstances.
5. God made the covenant with him
(indirectly).

How do we apply this for ourselves under
the New Covenant?

1. God initiated it all.
2. We need to make sure that we
have a heart's desire to
understand the ways of God.
3. God has given us clear promises in
Christ Jesus.
4. We have to choose to believe God
against all circumstances.
5. Through the finished work of the
cross, God made the
covenant with us (indirectly).

Chapter 15

The Absoluteness of the New Covenant

A covenant, even though it includes promises, is different from a promise. The New Covenant is even better than grace, which I will show you later. As we begin to grasp the wonder of this amazing New Covenant, we must still choose to believe in it with all of our heart. Remember, a covenant is a legal bond between two parties that outlines how they relate to each other. Therefore, in the New Covenant, God legally bound Himself to us and cannot relate to us in any other way than outlined in this covenant. If He did, it would violate His righteous nature, and, therefore, He would not be God anymore. I certainly would not want to have anything to do with a God who is a liar. Therefore, this New Covenant is absolute and even more certain than the daily rising of the sun.

I just prayed for a woman who was seriously sick. As I entered her room and talked to her about faith and divine healing, she told me that she believed in healing, but that God is free to do whatever He wants to do. As these words came out of her mouth, something hit me in my heart. I realized that this is a very common Old Covenant mentality, which I constantly meet. We throw the ball into God's court—but in fact He threw it into our court at that moment when Jesus said, "It is finished," and God made a New Covenant with us. I told the lady that God is not free anymore to do what He wants to do because He already bound Himself to us by a covenant. By choice, He gave up His freedom to deal with us in any other way than through Christ. Jesus paid for our miracles on the cross; now it is up to us to take them by appropriating faith or not. In the same way that God is not free anymore to choose who to save— people choose to take the salvation by faith that Christ paid for—He is also not free to relate to us in any other way but through Christ Jesus as long as we continue in the faith of the wonderful New Covenant.

God will relate to us in no way other than what He outlined in the New Covenant. Neither can we relate to God in any other way. You might think that this is common knowledge for every Christian, but I will prove to you that most Christians still try to relate to God on their own terms.

The reason why God cannot relate to us in any other manner is because His whole nature and character stands behind the Covenant. Do you remember that one of the attributes of His glory is faithfulness? We must keep reminding ourselves that a covenant is a bond by which God bound Himself to us, and there is no way out of it for Him. If God related to us or accepted us relating to Him in any other way, His perfect and righteous nature would be in question. God would then not be reliable anymore.

Three Reasons Why This Covenant Is Absolute

Please forgive me for repeating myself, but I did warn you that I would do so in the introduction of this book. I truly desire for these truths to be deeply ingrained into every fiber of your being. The first reason why this Covenant is absolute is that it was God's original plan.

Some people have the strange idea that the cross was God's plan B because man failed. But that is not the truth as we will clearly see from the Bible. The New Covenant has always been in the heart of God. The New Covenant is a perfect relationship between God and man without any interference of sin in that perfect harmony and intimacy. God never did have any other plan. Even though intimacy and harmony with God was destroyed through the sin of man, God did not come up with the idea of the New Covenant after sin entered the world. Let us look at Romans 16:25–26:

> Now to Him who is able to establish you according to my gospel and the preaching of Jesus Christ, according to the revelation of the mystery kept secret since the world began but now made manifest, and by the prophetic Scriptures made known to all nations, according to the commandment of the everlasting God, for obedience to the faith—

We understand that the gospel is the good news of the New Covenant. It was always God's plan; we just did not know it because it was hidden from us. Paul says here that this revelation was kept secret since the world began, which means it was already there; it was just hidden. With our limited understanding, we often have the warped idea that things have their origin with God when we receive the revelation about those things. For instance, over the last few years, many preachers all around the world are preaching the gospel with a strong emphasis on the message of grace. A good number of people have told me how wonderful it is that God is now bringing this revelation to the Church. They believe that because they now understand it that God is just now coming up with it.

God is not just now coming up with these new revelations of the gospel of grace. He wrote it into the Bible thousands of years ago. From all eternity, it has been His plan, and trust me, when God has a plan, He will make sure it is fulfilled. Paul tells us in another verse that the New Covenant has always been the plan of God:

> But we speak the wisdom of God in
> a mystery, the hidden wisdom which
> God ordained before the ages for
> our glory . . .
>
> —1 CORINTHIANS 2:7

Let me reassure you that anything that has always been in the heart of God is absolute.

The second reason why this covenant is absolute is because it does not depend on us. The Old Covenant did not just depend on God; it depended on God and man. God was never the problem; man always was. In His love, God entered into a radical New Covenant with us that removed every possibility of the covenant failing. The only way to do that was to remove the element of possible human failure. The writer to the Hebrews tells us that the New Covenant is not like the old one, which, of course, was not absolute because of the human element involved. We know that every chain is only as strong as the weakest link, and every relationship only as strong as the weakest party involved.

Since the New Covenant only depends on God and His Son Jesus, it is absolute. They both have already completed their respective parts in this covenant. When Jesus shouted the famous words, "It is finished," the meaning was "completely completed and nothing can be added to it," If you and I had to add our parts to this covenant, it would not be absolute because as we know, we have all failed, many times. This statement, "It is finished," is just one word in the original Greek language, *tetelestai,* from the root word, *teleó.*[1] It was used in various ways in ancient times, but I just want to mention here the ones that are important for us.

During a time of battle, a general would stand at the top of a hill where he could watch the entire conflict raging. Remember, there was no Air Force, tanks, or military vehicles at that time. Most of the fighting was done man-to-man with swords drawn. The soldiers were unable to see the entire battle; they were just concerned about killing any enemy near themselves. The general, who was standing upon the hill, clearly saw when the enemy was defeated or retreating, and at the point of victory, he shouted, *"It is finished!"* It was then the soldiers knew that it was all over, and the victory was theirs.

Another way *"It is finished"* was used was when someone made a business deal with a merchant and had a big debt to pay. When the very last payment was made, the merchant would take the bill and with big letters write across it, *"It is finished!"* This meant that the debt was paid in full, and there was no more payment to be made, ever.

The last way this word was used concerns prisoners. When a Roman citizen was convicted of a crime, he was thrown into prison. A certificate with his name, showing all of his crimes, was nailed to his prison cell door so that everyone walking by could see it. When he had served his full prison sentence, he had to appear again before the judge with that paper in his hand. The judge would then write across it, *"It is finished!"* That document was handed to the prisoner, and if anyone questioned why he was out of prison, all he had to do was to show the document. He was free.

It is vital that we understand the grammar in which this extremely important statement, *"It is finished!"* was written. The grammatical structure is in the *perfect, passive indicative.* The *perfect* tense indicates that the progress of an action has been completed and the result of that action *is ongoing and with full effect.* This means that as long as you exist, you will always experience the result of these powerful words if you can only grasp it by appropriating faith.

The *passive* voice indicates that *the subject of the sentence is being acted upon.* Jesus did not do anything to defend Himself; in fact, He was the perfect lamb that was slain without opening His mouth. Imagine how hard it must have been for Him, knowing that there were legions of angels at His disposal to defend and protect Him—or at least to ease the pain a little bit—but He refused any short cuts and remained passive.

The *indicative* mood indicates *a statement of fact or an actual occurrence from the speaker's perspective.* While this may sound like more of a grammar lesson than most readers care for, this information is, again, very important to understanding the significance of Jesus' words. What Jesus said was that the price for your sin being paid in full is a *FACT*, which nobody can change, not even you! The battle is over, the victory has been won, and you can now enter into the rest of God with your debt fully paid.

Let me show you several Bible verses that demonstrate to us what both God the Father and Jesus the Son did in order to make this covenant absolute. Hebrews 6:13–20 gives us a beautiful description of this fact□□□□□□□□□□□□□□□□□□□□□□□□□□□□□□□ □□□□□□□□□□□□□□□□□□□□□□□□□□□□□□□:

For when God made a promise to Abraham, because He could swear by no one greater, He swore by Himself, saying, "Surely blessing I will bless you, and multiplying I will multiply you." And so, after he had patiently endured, he obtained the promise. *For men indeed swear by the greater, and an oath for confirmation is for them an end of all dispute.* Thus God,

determining to show more abundantly to the heirs of promise the immutability of His counsel, confirmed it by an oath, that by two immutable things, in which *it is impossible for God to lie,* we might have strong consolation, who have fled for refuge to lay hold of the hope set before us. This hope we have as an anchor of the soul, both sure and steadfast, and which enters the Presence behind the veil, where the forerunner has entered for us, even Jesus, having become High Priest forever according to the order of Melchizedek. (Emphasis mine)

We see here that in verse 16 in the context of a covenant, an oath is the end of every dispute: "For men indeed swear by the greater, and an oath for confirmation is for them an end of all dispute." God swore when He made this Covenant; therefore, it is the end of every single dispute. This covenant cannot and never will fail. This is another picture of John 19:30: "It is finished!" Regardless of what arguments fill the minds and hearts of people regarding why this perfect covenant might also fail, let me tell you God's point of view:

it is the end of every dispute; it is a done deal; it is absolute because He swore. We also see in verse 17 that God was determined to show the immutability of His counsel:

> Thus God, determining to show more abundantly to the heirs of promise the immutability of His counsel, confirmed it by an oath . . .

In this verse, there are three key words—*determined, immutability,* and *heirs of promise*—which make this New Covenant so absolute. In simple words, the Bible is saying that God made an absolutely determined decision that His plan to give us the New Covenant was unchangeable and even our human failure could not annul it. Next, we see in verse 18 that it is impossible for God to lie:

> . . . that by two immutable things, in which it is impossible for God to lie, we might have strong consolation, who have fled for refuge to lay hold of the hope set before us. (Emphasis mine)

When I ask people if they believe in the omnipotence of God, they always answer in the affirmative. When I ask them what it means, they

tell me that God can do absolutely everything. I then tell them I do not believe that He can. To which they always respond with astonishment. I am very glad, however, that there is something that is impossible for God to do, which is to lie. Our New Covenant was given to us with a promise and an oath, and since God cannot lie, it is absolute. We also see in verses 19 to 20 that Jesus went ahead of us:

This hope we have as *an anchor of the soul, both sure and steadfast,* and which enters the Presence behind the veil, where the forerunner has entered for us, even Jesus, having become High Priest forever according to the order of Melchizedek. (Emphasis mine)

Jesus went inside the Holy of Holies into the very presence of God with His own precious blood and sealed this Covenant. In this verse we are told that this hope is an anchor for our souls; it is sure and steadfast. In other words, you never have to worry again that God's New Covenant could fail just because you fail. Jesus Himself made sure it is absolute.

We must understand that blood has a voice. Hebrews 12:24 says, "To Jesus the Mediator of the new covenant and to the *blood* of sprinkling *that speaks* better things than that of Abel" (emphasis mine). The Bible says that the life is in the blood, and life always has a voice.

Since Jesus entered into the most Holy Place with His own blood, that blood speaks constantly on our behalf. If the enemy accuses or condemns you, if your own brothers and sisters accuse and condemn you, or even if you condemn yourself, you can rest assured that the voice of the blood of Jesus drowns out every other voice of accusation and condemnation before the throne of your Father, who loves you so passionately and accepted the blood of His own Son on your behalf.

Revelation 12:11 says, "And they overcame him by the blood of the Lamb and by the word of their testimony, and they did not love their lives to the death." This speaks about overcoming the devil. He cannot stand against the blood of Jesus because it speaks against him and screams into his face, "You are a defeated foe; you are a loser and a liar!" We must believe with all of our hearts that the blood of Jesus constantly speaks on our behalf.

We have seen certain things that God and Jesus did, which made this Covenant absolute. Let me now show you one last thing that Jesus did, which is a beautiful illustration of "It is finished!" In Hebrews 10:11–12, we see that Jesus sat down:

> And every priest *stands* ministering daily and offering repeatedly the same sacrifices, which can never take away sins. But this Man, after He had offered one sacrifice for sins forever, *sat down* at the right hand of God . . . (Emphasis mine)

The context speaks of the New Covenant, comparing it with the Old Covenant. I want you to pay attention to two words, *stands* and *sat*. We are told that every High Priest stands, ministering daily. The High Priest was never allowed to sit down because he had to bring continual sacrifices for the people under the Old Covenant. Here we are told that after Jesus offered His sacrifice, He sat down. "It is finished." The covenant is absolute.

The third reason why the New Covenant is absolute is because it was made between God the Father and Jesus His Son. We know that God is eternally faithful and Jesus will never fail. We are told that Jesus Christ will remain the same yesterday, today, and forever (Heb. 13:8). Neither God nor Jesus will ever disappoint or fail the other, which makes the New Covenant absolute.

God, out of His deep love for us, made sure that there would be an eternal covenant that would never fail. This Covenant simply depends on our faith in the finished work of the cross. Any time you try to come to God or relate to Him outside the boundaries of this New Covenant, you are unable to experience all of the covenant's blessings. This does not mean you have lost your salvation, but it does mean that you are unable to experience and enjoy the benefits of what Christ did for you on the cross.

Endnote

1. *teleó*, "to bring to an end, complete, fulfill"; Strong's #5055; http://biblehub.com/greek/5055.htm; accessed 19 June 2017.

Chapter 16

The New Covenant Supersedes Grace

I am fully aware that the above statement sounds very controversial. With my mind's eye, I can already see stones being thrown at me from different groups of people within the Church. Is grace not the central message of the gospel? Is grace not this radical, wonderful, new way in which God relates to us? Is grace not the unmerited favor of God? I will explain to you from the Bible why the New Covenant supersedes grace. Although grace is a part of the New Covenant, it is not the same thing.

Grace is generally understood in the Christian world as the undeserved favor of God. I personally do not like it when we give this definition of grace since it is not biblically accurate. To simply say that grace is the unmerited favor of God is limiting grace. It is only one of the many aspects of grace, but it is not what grace is in its fullest meaning. Grace includes the ability to lift us above our circumstances and serve the Lord with endurance and diligence as seen in 1 Corinthians 15:10. Grace is also the supernatural, divine ability that gives us the power not to sin (Rom. 6:14). Grace is also the ability to give financially more than what we would naturally be able to give, according to 2 Corinthians 8:1–2.

It is true, however, that one of the definitions of grace is God's favor, which cannot be deserved or earned, only freely received. Although the New Covenant includes grace, it supersedes it by far. Grace is not just a New Testament word or concept as many believe. We can find this word in the Old Testament too. We are told in Exodus 33:17 that Moses found grace with God:

> So the LORD said to Moses, "I will also do this thing that you have spoken; for you have found grace in My sight, and I know you by name."

Here we see a man, living under the Old Covenant, yet finding grace in God's sight. People have this false idea that grace did not start until Jesus Christ came into this world. The first mention of grace is thousands of years ago when the Bible says in Genesis 6:8, "But Noah found grace in the eyes of the LORD."

Let's examine why the New Covenant supersedes grace; it is an important topic. The example of Moses above will begin to answer this question. Although Moses found grace in the eyes of the Lord, God did not permit him to enter the Promised Land. How could the Promised Land be withheld from someone who found grace in the eyes of the Lord? In this very question, we find the answer to why the New Covenant supersedes grace. God can give His grace to whomever He chooses to, whenever He chooses to. Since He can give it freely by His own choice, He can also retrieve it. In the New Covenant, God bound Himself in an absolute, certain way to deal with us in a specific manner that can never be changed. It is finished!

In other words, God bound Himself through the New Covenant in such a way that He cannot remove His kindness from us no matter what we do (Isa. 54:8, 10). Let us look at another example from the Old Testament where it talks about grace. In Ezra 9:8, we read,

> And now *for a little while grace has been shown* from the LORD our God, to leave us a remnant to escape, and to give us a peg in His holy place, that our God may enlighten our eyes and give us a measure of revival in our bondage. (Emphasis mine)

Here we clearly see that grace had been shown only for a period of time, which makes it inferior to the New Covenant. I am not belittling grace or trying to say that it is not important since it is included in the New Covenant. I simply want to show you that God, in His kindness, has given us something better than just grace. While grace can be given or withheld, even retrieved again once given as we see in the life of Moses, in the New Covenant, God bound Himself to Jesus Christ in an unfailing covenant and can never retrieve it. Our covenant is not limited in time, but is eternal as seen in Hebrews 13:20:

> Now may the God of peace who brought up our Lord Jesus from the dead, that great Shepherd of the sheep, through the blood of the *everlasting covenant. . .* (Emphasis mine)

This is the final and everlasting covenant that God has entered into with people. Without a covenant, God can choose to deal with us in any way that He would like to. He could treat us however He chooses, and He could even treat different people in different ways. Because of His own righteous character and nature, once

He enters this covenant, He has no other choice but to deal with us according to the way He bound Himself in that covenant. This is the reason why the New Covenant supersedes grace. Under this covenant, He must treat everyone equally, according to how He outlined it in the covenant.

÷ authority *giving Glory the power*

This is why I believe *clericalism,* which many churches still practice today, is a doctrine from hell. It violates the heart of the New Covenant. God does not treat me, as one who has faithfully served Him for more than 35 years, any differently than the person who has been the filthiest, most rotten sinner and just got saved today. They might not have learned yet how to use the right language in prayer or how to act righteously according to their new nature; however, if they approach God based on His eternal covenant with them, which starts the moment they enter into it by faith, they can exercise the same authority that I exercise.

God cannot treat individuals differently because He bound Himself to us in this eternal, unbreakable covenant. If the Church could only grasp this, it would be the end of clericalism and fighting for position, and every member would be a minister who expresses boldness before God and brings heaven to earth. You must never allow the thought and attitude that the prayer of certain people (or, in your opinion, special men or women of God) has more authority before God than your own prayer does. This is Old Covenant thinking which will limit the victory in your life and must be rejected vehemently!

The Mystical Union

A key to understanding the New Covenant and experiencing all of its benefits is to fully understand a mystical union. By faith in the finished work of the cross of Jesus Christ, we become totally united with Him and enter into a mystical union with Him, which makes us partakers of every benefit of this Covenant. Two very important things have changed through this unity: everything that belongs to Jesus now also belongs to us; and God will only relate to us through who we are in Christ. Suddenly, abiding in Christ has a totally new, deep, and important meaning. Phrases like "in Christ" or "in Him" are key words in the New Covenant and are found eighty-eight times in the New Testament. I encourage and challenge you to carefully study the New Testament and find out every time it uses either of these phrases.

When I was a young man, I took a brand-new Bible and circled every time it said one of the above phrases. We must keep in mind that only through appropriating faith will the promises become ours by experience. I will talk more about this later.

Since the key to the New Covenant is that God made it with Jesus and we enter into it by faith, we must become sure about our identity in Jesus. God will not relate to us according to our past, our present, or our future. He will only relate to us through who we are in Christ because the covenant is between God and Jesus, and we must abide in Him to enjoy all the amazing benefits of this covenant.

Abiding in Him has nothing to do with works but with resting in the finished work of the cross. It means that we firmly believe in our heart that the day we repented from our sin and believed in the death of Jesus for our sin, we entered this mystical union, and now we are one with Him. We are in Christ, and Christ is in us! Look at what Colossians 1:27 says,

> To them God willed to make known what are the riches of the glory of this mystery among the Gentiles:

which is Christ in you, the hope of glory.

Christ is in you! What an amazing truth. Add to this the fact that He is not going to leave you, not even when you sin, because He promised that He will never leave us nor forsake us (Heb. 13:5). Sin in our lives will not break our relationship with God. However, sin will disrupt our intimacy with Him. God is a covenant-keeping God, but when we sin, our intimacy with Him is broken, not because He has broken it, but because our own hearts are affected by sin and God is a heart-God who relates to us from His heart to ours.

Since God made His eternal covenant with Jesus and not directly with us (we only entered into it because of faith), He can relate to us in no other way except through Christ. What happened when we believed? We came into Christ, and Christ came into us as we saw in the above scripture. Now carefully read, study, and meditate on this truth. God only relates to us through Christ. Christ has God's favor; therefore, we also have God's favor because we are in Him. God looks at Reinhard (put your name here), but He does not see Reinhard; He sees Jesus because I am in Him. Since this is the only way He is allowed to relate to me under the

New Covenant because He bound Himself by an oath, He says, "You have all My favor."

Then the devil points to stuff in my heart and accuses me and tries to condemn me as I come before God. God already sees me in Christ, but the devil tells me, "Yes, you are in Christ, but inside of you is so much garbage." Then God looks inside of me and what does He see? According to Colossians 1:27 which we read above, God sees Christ. So now He says, "Christ has my favor. Since He is in you, and you are in Him, I have no option but to give you double favor because I am in a covenant with Christ in you, and also with you in Christ!" But of course, if you try to relate to God in any other way than through Christ, you cannot enjoy and experience God's favor. This is why Paul concludes 1 Corinthians 1:31, after He says that we are in Christ, with this statement: "As it is written, 'He who glories, let him glory in the Lord.'"

My beloved friend, renounce all of your good works which you want to use to relate to God. Reject your past, your achievements, your boasting, your success, and your failures as a basis of relating to the Lord. Glory in the Lord, the One who sealed this eternal covenant! It is finished!

Neither the old Reinhard nor the old you exists any longer because we are in Christ. Second Corinthians 5:17 tells us,

> Therefore, if anyone is in Christ, he is a new creation; old things have passed away; behold, all things have become new.

The word *new* means unprecedented, brand-new, never seen before. We are so united with Jesus that we could say human beings like us have never been seen before. Unfortunately, many Christians do not believe this truth simply because they do not experience it. Christian life does not work like that. You must not have the attitude, "God show me, and I will believe You," because God sets the terms of how we are to relate to Him, and He said, "Believe Me, and I will show you"! We have reversed the order, and that is why we do not experience many of the amazing benefits of the New Covenant.

I recently prayed for a twenty-year-old young lady in another country who had so many sicknesses and pains it was incredible. As I laid my hands on her to pray for a miracle, the Holy Spirit said to me that the reason for all her pain was that she worried herself sick. I wanted to be kind and loving to her, so I did not tell her what the Spirit said to me; instead, I asked her if she worried a lot. She told me that she worried about every little thing from morning until night. Then I told her that God showed me that she made herself sick and that if I were to pray at that time and she received a miracle, she would be in the same trouble again soon because of her worrying. I told her that I would quickly teach her how to live a worry-free life, and then I would pray for her miracle.

Her dad was standing next to me and quickly jumped in, telling me that she could not help it because the problem ran in her genes; it was hereditary. Her mom worried, her grandma worried, their parents worried . . . I put my hand right up close in front of his mouth and said something like this, "Stop, I don't care how many generations have worried themselves sick; she now has a brand-new identity and brand-new genes. Her new Father is in heaven, and He never worries about anything. She carries His DNA and has a right to experience it." I prayed for her, and she said she felt some relief. I have not yet been back to that area to hear about the end of the story.

God will not relate to you on the basis of your past, natural DNA, religion, good works, or failures. He bound Himself in this amazing New Covenant to only relate to you through Christ. By faith alone are you in Christ; therefore, do not come before God on any other basis. When you stand before Him, He sees Jesus, perfect, pure, holy, and deserving health, provision, protection, and every spiritual blessing. The problem is that people try to relate to God in all sorts of different ways, just not in who they are in Christ! It is truly finished!

Chapter 17

Appropriating Faith

Recently, the Lord said to me that one of His great sorrows is the lack of appropriating faith in the life of His children. The subject of true, biblical faith has fascinated me since my childhood. But on that particular night, the Lord spoke to me using the word *appropriating* concerning faith, and that word really caught my attention. I also sensed urgency as well as a deep sadness in His heart. Therefore, I asked Him to explain it to me further.

As the Lord kindly began to reveal His heart to me, I started to weep in His presence. He told me that the lack of appropriating faith in the life of His children is a defiance of the cross of His Son. He revealed to me the intense pain of the cross and the high price that His Son had to pay for us to be able to receive so many wonderful benefits. Our lack of appropriating faith would be like smacking Jesus in the face as He hung on the cross.

The Old Covenant mentality was about God responding to our faith; that put the emphasis *on our faith*. In the New Covenant, our faith *is a response* to the finished work of the cross, which puts the emphasis on what *Jesus did*, not on us or *our* faith. In the Old Covenant, they believed and looked forward to what God would do in response to their faith. We, in the New Covenant, do not look forward but back, in faith, to what happened almost 2000 years ago when Jesus shouted, *"It is finished!"*

Appropriating faith means faith that receives. Receiving, in the language of the Bible, is different than what receiving means in the minds of many people. There are different Hebrew and Greek words used for *receiving* in the Bible. But when Scripture talks about receiving things in prayer, it uses a word that means to lay hold of with our hands and not to let go. Appropriating faith never asks God to give to us what already belongs to us through the New Covenant. It lays hold of it by faith, which is expressed through thanksgiving, and begins to act like it already has what was asked for without seeing it yet in the natural world. It never looks at feelings or is influenced by circumstances.

Appropriating faith *never complains about anything* because it understands that complaining is one of the greatest signs of unbelief and is a very destructive behavior in the life of a New Covenant Christian. If God truly has given us all things through Christ, and we still complain about our circumstances, it shows an attitude of unbelief in our hearts. Therefore, when I teach about the New Covenant, I like to exhort people strongly to remove all complaining from their lives.

Let me give you an example to help you understand. God told me in 2004 to leave everything behind in Austria, to take my wife and my children, and to move to the USA. In the natural, that made no sense, since we had all the security we needed in Austria and had nothing in the USA. We had no property to sell, no money in the savings account, nothing that was of any significant value. I had no job in the USA, and it all looked totally uncertain. As the time of our moving to the USA came closer and many things had not yet been worked out, I started to feel a bit anxious. We tried to find a renter for our apartment, which belonged to the government, in order to sell some of our furniture to them. But it was complicated because the rules and regulations for who would be allowed to take over our apartment were complex.

Then God spoke to me one night, saying that it was a done deal since He had promised me that He would never leave me nor forsake me. I never prayed another prayer after that night; I didn't do another thing to find a renter, nor did I move a finger to make anything else happen. I simply praised the Lord for the done deal; I kept thanking Him and acted like it was all settled. I was even called stupid and irresponsible by some of my friends. Instead of trying to fix my problem, I took my lovely wife to Switzerland for three days to celebrate our wedding anniversary. While I was in Switzerland, God supernaturally took care of everything, and it ended up being absolutely perfect. That is appropriating faith. If I had kept praying, kept pleading with God to help me, kept trying to sort it all out, nothing would have happened. Appropriating faith takes hold of what belongs to us through thanksgiving and praise, and then begins to act like it is a done deal.

These following pages are so important for you to understand if you truly want to experience the New Covenant. I ask you to read them slowly and carefully; meditate on these words over and over again. Maybe you will have to read them many times. Ask the Holy Spirit to help you to understand these words. Tell Him your desire to experience every aspect of the New Covenant. Ask God to give you the Spirit of wisdom and revelation as well as to open the eyes of your heart to these truths.

Promises and "God-Facts"

In my book *Faith,* I talk about the difference between facts and truth. I explain that a truth is stronger than a fact and we have to choose to believe it. For instance, it is a fact of the law of physics that people cannot walk on water. However, the Gospels tell a story about Peter walking on water. He did so believing the truth over the fact. Everything that Jesus says is the truth because He is the truth, according to John 14:6. Consequently, if we make a choice to believe the truth over the facts, we will experience the supernatural. In Peter's case, the fact was that you cannot walk on water, but the truth was that Jesus said he could and he did. Maybe the fact is that a doctor told you that there is no cure for you or that your circumstances tell you there is no hope. You must choose to believe the truth of the Word of God over the facts you see in the natural.

There are not just natural facts; there is also something that I am calling God-facts. God-facts are different from God's promises. God-facts are directly related to the New Covenant. Promises have to do with the future while God-facts have to do with the past, with what happened at the cross about two-thousand years ago. When Jesus shouted, "It is finished," He released certain God-facts into the spiritual world for us to take hold of by appropriating faith.

A God-fact is not something God promises that He will do (which would be in the future); it is something that God said He already did (which is in the past). There is only one way that God ordained for us to experience them, which is by appropriating faith. We do not receive them by the intercession of other people, or by the laying on of hands of a man of God, or even by fasting and praying. We have to claim them instead of asking for them. We must thank God that they belong to us and act as if they are already ours because "It is finished." Appropriating faith thanks God for the God-facts and acts as though they are ours because they truly are.

To help you better understand this truth, let me illustrate it for you. If you ask God to give you victory over some particular sin, you will never experience that victory. You can have the most anointed man of God pray for you, and you can fast and pray for extended periods of time—and still not receive the victory. Victory over sin is a God-fact, which means it is something that has happened in the past and must be appropriated by us through faith alone.

If you study Romans 6:7–8, you will clearly see that these facts are stated. Romans 6:2 says, "We are dead to sin." Verse eleven says that we must reckon ourselves to be dead to sin. Romans 8:2 says that the law of the Spirit of life in Christ Jesus has made us free from the law of sin and death. And Paul says in Galatians 2:20 that we have been crucified with Christ. All of these are God-facts of the New Covenant, which you must believe, declare, and thank God for in order to see them manifest in your life and receive the victory. If you ask God to crucify your flesh or put all your effort into it, you will experience nothing but defeat, defying the cross because of your lack of appropriating faith.

Praying and asking God to give us these God-facts, as well as asking other people for prayer that God would give them to us, is a sign of a lack of knowledge or of unbelief—both of which will withhold these wonderful blessings from us. God does not withhold them, but since they can only be received by appropriating faith, there is nothing that God can do anymore for us.

When we do not see these things manifest in our lives because of our religious and wrong beliefs, we start to put the blame on God and ask why He did not respond to our prayers. We end up with a wrong and distorted picture of God, and our intimate relationship with Him is severed. Oh, how I hate religion! I have had much resistance in my Christian life because I firmly believe in this principle and practice it. I have confronted many religious sayings in the church that go directly against God-facts and the New Covenant. It is such a common practice among Christians today to constantly ask God for things that He has already given us in Christ. This must stop.

Allow me to illustrate this with something that will help you grab hold of this important truth.

Imagine that you are in a difficult situation in your life. You are facing difficulties and circumstances that do not allow you to experience the fullness of life that Jesus promised when He said that He came to give us abundant life (John10:10). You begin to pray, ask other people to pray for you, pray more intensely, and eventually add fasting to your prayers. You ask God to give you strength, change your circumstances, and whatever else you feel you need for the victory.

Now, neither prayer, nor fasting, nor others praying for us, are in themselves bad things. However, to do these things with regard to God-facts truly is a bad thing because by our wrong action we turn the God-fact, which is in the present, into a promise which now is in the future. It will never be ours; however, it will remain in the future. God-facts are past-tense actions (things that have already happened) while promises are future-tense actions (things we are still waiting and hoping for).

What is happening then? Why is your prayer not answered? Why does God not respond to you? Why does He seem to ignore your prayers and the prayers of others? Frustration sets in, and eventually you are so discouraged that you give up, maybe even on God. Then one day at the end of your life you die and stand before Jesus. Jesus welcomes you to heaven and asks if there are any questions you have regarding your life on earth. You have been waiting for this opportunity since you never got an answer to something specific that you were waiting for while you lived on earth. You pour out your heart, telling Him that you felt so disappointed and let down because in your time of real need, He did not respond to you and give you victory so that you could live an abundant life as He promised you.

With a smile and a heart of compassion, Jesus takes your hand, and you walk together to a huge warehouse. You walk through the door, and there are hundreds of shelves, loaded with every possible thing you can imagine. You see exactly what you had asked Him for while you walked through your crises. You say, "Jesus, here is the strength that I asked you to give me." Then you point to the next shelf and say, "And here is the victory I fasted and prayed for. Why did You not give it to me?" Jesus smiles and says to you, "My dearly beloved child, do you not remember the New Covenant? In it, My Father bound Himself legally to you and determined the only way that we were to relate to you and you were to relate to us. We clearly wrote into the Bible, which we gave you, all the things that we had already given to you through the New Covenant. The moment we gave them to you, we deposited them into this warehouse. They were no longer ours to give, but yours to take!"

Then He takes you outside that warehouse and points to the front of it. As you look up, you see a huge sign on the warehouse, which has your name on it. You look at Him with tears in your eyes because you now understand. You remember that He wrote in 2 Peter 1:3, "As His divine power has given to us all things that pertain to life and godliness, through the knowledge of Him who called us by glory and virtue." He nods at you with His perfect eyes of love and compassion and says, "Yes, my beloved child, we deposited all things that you ever needed for an abundant life into your warehouse here when I died on the cross and sealed the New Covenant. I saw you praying, asking, pleading, fasting, and begging, but there was nothing I could do. These things belong neither to My Father nor to Me; they were yours, and, therefore, we could not give them to you. The warehouse has your name on it; we would have had to steal them from your warehouse to get them to you, and neither My Father nor I am a thief."

My dear friend, I hope you understand this picture and from now on, will constantly enter boldly into your warehouse in heaven to grab all of your God-facts and live a life of perfect victory that glorifies God and honors the wonderful New Covenant. When I arrive in heaven, I want to find an empty warehouse with my name on it!

It is vital for us to understand that when we approach God in prayer, we must not try to *convince Him* of anything. He already has given us all things through Christ. He is constantly working so hard to *convince us* to simply use appropriating faith and enjoy the beautiful New Covenant. One minute of appropriating faith in the finished work of the cross avails much more than an entire night of crying out to God in hope.

As I am writing this, I am just returning from a trip to Poland where a couple shared their testimony with me; it made me cry because I was so touched. They have been married for six years and were unable to have children. They prayed and cried out to God with no results. They were convinced that they believed, but found out through my teaching that they did not truly have faith, but were living in hope. The wife spent two months meditating on some wonderful God-facts—including that children are a blessing from God and that we have been blessed with every spiritual blessing—until her heart finally believed these God-facts. Two weeks after her meditation months, she found out she was pregnant. Now they want the whole world to know how wonderful life in the New Covenant really is.

Chapter 18

Detecting "God-Facts"

When the Lord told me that night that the lack of appropriating faith in the lives of His children is one of His greatest sorrows, it impacted me very deeply for several reasons. I remember moments in my own life when I did not walk in that kind of faith and was, therefore, defying the work of the cross. I neither want to make the Lord sad, nor do I want to defy the work of the cross, which cost Jesus so much. I dare not say that I walk perfectly in this appropriating faith now, but as Paul said, "One thing I do, I forget what is behind me and press on towards the goal!" As we have seen, God-facts are fairly easy to detect in the New Testament. They are either written in a certain grammar or else use words like "in Him," "in Christ," or "in Jesus."

Understanding Biblical Grammar

It is amazing how prone we are to either ignore or misunderstand the simplest grammar rules, which even most children can understand. There is the present tense, which means that an action is happening right now in the present. There is the present-continuous tense, which means an action is happening right now and will continue to happen. Next, there is the future tense, which means an action has not yet happened, but will happen. Finally, there is the past tense, which is an action that has been completed in the past; nothing can be added to it, nor can it be changed.

The God-facts in the Bible are easier to detect than many people realize. As I told, you they can be discovered by clue words or by their grammatical tense, which will always be in the past tense or possibly the present tense—but never in the future tense. If God-facts are in the present tense, they always have clue words like "in Him," "in Christ," or "through Him." Since we are in a perfect union with Jesus Christ through faith in the finished work of the cross, it is a God-fact that we have whatever He has. Look at this verse in 2 Corinthians which is in the present tense, but also includes the God-fact clue words:

> Now thanks be to God who always leads us in triumph *in Christ,* and through us diffuses the fragrance of His knowledge in every place. (Emphasis mine)
>
> —2 CORINTHIANS 2:14

Although this is not written in the past tense (a big God-fact clue), we do see the other God-fact clue, namely the words "in Christ." God "always leads us in triumph," meaning a celebration of victory in Christ. This is a New Covenant God-fact: because we are in Christ through the New Covenant, Christ's victory is our victory. All we have to do is to appropriate this God-fact by faith.

Allow me to illustrate how a past tense needs to be understood in the Bible. Recently, I traveled with a translator to a small town in the south of Brazil. The people of the church kept asking me what I wanted to eat, to which I replied, "I will eat anything." They truly tried to honor me and kept pressing me to tell them a certain kind of food that I would want them to make for me. Finally, I told them that I absolutely love fried yucca root (mandioca), especially when it is small and crunchy.

The mother of the pastor had a passion for cooking and entertaining people. That night, when we arrived at her house the table was overloaded with food. After I ate so much that I was overly full, she kept saying, "Pastor, you hardly ate anything; eat more," and kept putting more on my plate. My translator and I did not want to offend the lady, so we ate more. We got back to our hotel very late, long past midnight. Needless to say, neither of us felt well or slept very well at all.

Early the next morning, as I went to the meeting to teach about the New Covenant, I realized that I had just experienced a perfect illustration of a past tense. I wished I had not eaten that much greasy food that late at night. My stomach still felt terrible the next morning. This action could neither be changed nor could anything be added to nor subtracted from it because it was finished. My regrets did not alter the action from the night before or undo it because it was in the past tense.

Because of a lack of understanding of appropriating faith and of this simple grammatical rule as we read the Bible, we miss many things that belong to us. Jesus is our Covenant, as we see in Isaiah 42:6:

> I, the LORD, have called You in righteousness, and will hold Your hand; I will keep You and *give You as a covenant* to the people, as a light to the Gentiles (Emphasis mine)

Since Jesus is our Covenant, not a single one of these New Covenant God-facts can be experienced in any other way than by being in Him through faith alone and by claiming and taking hold of them by faith. We have to understand that it is union with Him and appropriating faith alone that lets us experience these wonderful benefits. I want to emphasize that appropriating faith does not make these benefits a fact; they already are facts through the New Covenant.

What changes with our appropriating faith is our experience, not what God does. We are not in Christ by works, only by faith; therefore, no amount of effort, holiness, good works, prayers, or fasting will give us the benefits of the New Covenant. We must abide in Him, which is not by effort or works, but by faith alone. How did we become united with Christ? Was it not by faith in the work of the cross? Since we came into Christ by faith, we also remain in Him by faith. Just believe that you are in Him!

Under the New Covenant, we have to learn to replace words like *ask, pray,* and *request* with *claim, declare,* and *thank.* Anything in the New Testament that has been written in the past tense or has any of the other God-fact clues, needs neither to be asked for, prayed for, or requested from God. Rather, we must boldly claim them, declare that they are ours, and thank God for them in order to receive them. Let me "plead with you by the mercies of God" not to give in to the temptation to ask God for anything that we have been told belongs to us. I understand that this will take a great paradigm shift in your mind and heart because of the mix of the Old and New Covenants that you have been accustomed to. I also ask you not to interpret anything in the Bible in any other way except through John 19:30, "It is finished."

What exactly does that last sentence mean? It means that in all the things that we experience in life or read in the Scriptures, we need to ask ourselves this question: "Did Jesus, through His death, burial, and resurrection, pay for what we are experiencing (or reading)? Did Jesus pay for our poverty or sickness?" The answer is obvious; He paid for us to be released from poverty and sickness. You can apply this in every area of your life. Never forget that God is by nature a covenant-keeping God. Since He bound Himself to us through His Son Jesus Christ, He will never relate to us in any other way. He, as the stronger partner, set the terms of the Covenant. We may accept them or reject them; these are the only two choices that we have.

A Practical Example

In the following example, I will illustrate to you how this covenant works. Imagine that the President of the United States makes a contract with a friend of his. This contract not only includes his friend but also anybody who will ever be a family member of that friend and carries the friend's name. In this contract, the President guarantees with all the authority and power of the United States of America that all protection, wealth, security, healthcare, and every other imaginable benefit belong to his friend. He signs the contract with the seal of the United States government, which means that it cannot be broken.

His friend moves into the White House in Washington, D.C., and enjoys having his own bodyguards, top chefs, as many massages as he wants, and the best doctors in the United States. Something unimaginable then happens; this friend visits Brazil and travels to the poorest area in the northeast. There he sees a young lady who lives on the trash heap. She has been abandoned and rejected as a baby; she never had any parents and grew up with no self-worth. He falls in love with her and decides to marry her. He brings her back to the USA in Air Force One, the official plane of the President. He moves her into the White House and tells her that everything she needs is hers for the taking.

Because of her past of abuse and poverty, she feels completely unworthy to live such an extravagant lifestyle. She is afraid that she will embarrass the President if she requests nice things. She, therefore, lives in a small room of the White House in sickness and poverty, simply because she does not understand that powerful contract. By marriage, she came into perfect union with the President's friend, who has a contract with the most powerful nation of the world. All the protection, security, wealth, and other benefits were already hers for the taking. There was never a contract made between the United States and her, only between the USA and her husband. She simply became the beneficiary by entering into a union with him.

Does this not sound a lot like the New Covenant? God, the Creator of the universe, enters into a covenant with His beloved Son, Jesus Christ, and allows us to become the beneficiaries by union with Jesus. Many of us never experience all that the New Covenant has given us because we do not understand or use appropriating faith by taking what is already ours through our union with Christ.

In the next chapter, I will show you God-facts that many Christians pray for and never receive. The reason is very simple: you cannot receive God-facts by asking for them; you must take them by faith. You simply recognize them as facts, as actions completed in the past, which can never be changed. Nothing can be added to them or taken from them. I cannot give you all of the God-facts in this book; therefore, I will only give you a select few. I trust that you will diligently search the Scriptures for yourself, asking the Holy Spirit to reveal others to you.

David tells us in Psalm 25:14 that "the secret of the LORD is with those who fear Him, and He will show them His covenant." What is the Lord's secret, if not His New Covenant with us? The condition for receiving this revelation is to fear Him, which has nothing to do with being afraid of Him. There are two Bible verses that illustrate wonderfully what it means to fear the Lord in the New Covenant. Deuteronomy 6:13 tells us, "You shall fear the LORD your God and serve Him." When Jesus was tempted by the devil in the wilderness, He quoted this very verse back to the devil, saying, "For it is written, 'You shall worship the LORD your God, and Him only shall you serve.'" (Luke 4:8) We see that to fear the Lord does not mean to be afraid of Him but to surrender to Him out of the desire of our heart, which is the true meaning of worship.

Chapter 19

Taking What Belongs to Us

As we have already seen, in order for us to experience all the God-facts, we have to stop asking for them and instead take them by appropriating faith. This is so important because anything you ask from God remains in the future until the moment you receive it here in your life. This may be sooner or later. Abraham had to wait for more than ten years to get his son. God chooses when He gives you what you requested; after all, He is God, and we have to fulfill the biblical conditions for receiving the promises of which one is perseverance. Hebrews 6:12 tells us,

> . . . that you do not become sluggish,
> but imitate those who through faith
> and patience inherit the promises.

We clearly see that patience, which in the original Greek means endurance or perseverance, is one of the conditions to receive the promises of God.[1] If you give up believing, you might never receive what God has for you. This is one of the keys for praying under the New Covenant because if you pray or ask God for any God-fact, it will never materialize. You may ask or pray for promises, but never for God-facts.

The first God-fact that I want to talk about is one that few Christians have learned to take, yet it is so clearly written in the Bible. Look at the following verse carefully, especially in the light of the difference between promises and God-facts:

> Blessed be the God and Father of our Lord Jesus Christ, who has blessed us with every spiritual blessing in the heavenly places in Christ.
>
> —EPHESIANS 1:3

Here we see both of the rules for finding a God-fact applied. It is written in the past tense, "has blessed," and the words "in Christ" are added. God could not have made it any clearer. What we read here has been given to us through the New Covenant. Maybe you think that you believe this verse. I learned many years ago that what you believe is never measured by what you say, but by how you act. If you truly believe this scripture, you would never again ask God for His blessing. You would also never again say to people, "God bless you."

I greatly dislike it when people say that to me. We constantly say to each other, "God bless you," without realizing what we are doing to each other by saying it. When people say to me, "God bless you," I usually do not say anything because I want to show love and respect and understand that they have not yet learned how to fully walk in the New Covenant. Once I teach people about the New Covenant, I ask them to never say those words to me again. Since you have obviously almost read the entire book, I am now asking you, should you ever meet me somewhere, please do not say to me, "God bless you."

Why is this so important to me? The explanation is very simple; God-facts can only be experienced in our lives by appropriating faith, which means that you must stop asking for it. You must claim it, thank God for it, and act like it is absolutely true because it is. As long as I ask God to bless you or me, it is something that remains in the future. What I am ultimately saying is that He has not yet blessed us, and I am wishing that He would do so. This defies the work of the cross and the New Covenant.

Recently, a pastor tried to convince me that the Bible teaches us that we should bless one another. When I challenged Him to give me proof by showing me a verse where it says we should bless each other under the New Covenant, he could only point to a couple of scriptures which proved my point. The only time we are told in the New Testament to bless each other is in regards to our enemies in Matthew 5 and to people who do bad things to us in 1 Peter 3:9. These scriptures never tell us that we should ask God to bless these people, but that we should bless them. The implication is very clear; we must demonstrate the heart and unconditional love of the Father to those who deserve it the least.

The Example of Bill Gates

I want to illustrate this to you through an example that can easily be understood. At the time of the writing of this book, Bill Gates, the founder of Microsoft, is currently the richest man in the world. Imagine that I meet him somewhere and he makes a choice that I will be his new best friend. I am a simple person who has never had a lot of money, and I live a simple life. When Bill Gates offers me his friendship, he also gives me his credit card and says, "This is now yours." Something interesting just took place; I have been blessed with every resource that Bill Gates has. In the same way that Bill Gates has given me his resources and welcomed me into the circle of his own friends, all the blessings of the spiritual world have been given to me because I have been received into God's family by being in Christ Jesus.

I go home to my apartment and tell my wife, full of excitement, that I am the new best friend of the richest man of the world. In great unbelief, my wife, Debi, tells me that I need to stop dreaming and come back to reality. I show her the credit card, to which she replies, "Where did you find that? You have to take it back." I try to convince her that Bill Gates himself gave it to me because I am now his new best friend. Still in disbelief, she says, "Did you steal it from him?" To which I reply, "No, he gave it to me."

The next day I am driving my car too fast and carelessly. I cause an accident, which is totally my fault. My car is destroyed, and I have no insurance to pay for a new car. I arrive at my house feeling shame and guilt, knowing that our family really needs a car. I keep telling my wife how sorry I am for what I did. She says to me, "Where is your new best friend now that you need him? Let's see what he will do for you now that you have messed up and are in trouble."

I do what most Christians do in their spiritual lives in relationship with God; I call Bill Gates, which is the equivalent to praying to God. When Bill answers the phone, I ask him if he remembers me, his new best friend. He gets very excited that I want to communicate with him. Apologetically, I explain the mess that I made. Full of guilt, shame, and self-pity, I tell him how badly I feel. Then in seeming (but false) humility, I ask him to buy me a car. I tell him that I am a simple and humble man and that a small, used car would be sufficient for me.

My wife stands next to me, carefully listening to what is happening. After Bill listens to me, he hangs up the phone without responding. I feel devastated and confused by his actions, wondering whether it was my carelessness that caused Bill to be so harsh with me. My wife asks me what happened to my new best friend; where is he when I truly need him? Bill is a few thousand miles away, sitting in his living room next to his wife, Melinda. She asks him if that was his new best friend. He answers, "Yes, and he is a very strange guy." Melinda wonders what the conversation was all about, and Bill tells her, "Yesterday I gave him my credit card and told him that it is now his. He refuses to use it but instead asks me for something I already gave him. It is impossible for me to give him any more than I have already given him, yet he still asks me for what I have already told him is his. There is nothing anymore I can do for him."

Now let us translate this story into the everyday life of a Christian. God clearly wrote into His Bible that He already has (which means a completed action that cannot be changed) blessed us with every single spiritual blessing in the heavenly places in Christ Jesus. Yet, we keep asking God to bless us, or we say to each other, "God bless you," which is a contradiction to His Word. God-facts are New Covenant truths that can only be experienced by taking what belongs to us; they will remain distant as long as we keep asking for them for ourselves or others.

This is a principle that must be applied regarding every single New Covenant God-fact. What I should have done, regarding my broken car, was to reject any guilt or shame, gone to the car dealer, demanded a car, put Bill Gates' credit card on the desk, and expressing thankfulness, I should have left. I would have had a brand-new car.

Let me explain to you how I apply this in my own personal life. I constantly thank God and praise Him that He has already blessed me with every spiritual blessing in the heavenly places in Christ Jesus. I boldly declare that I expect all of these blessings to manifest in my life today. I expect them to manifest in my health, in my service for Him, and in my relationships, as well as in every other area of my life. I walk in the experience of the finished work of the cross because I stopped asking and simply take what belongs to me.

When I "crash my car," meaning, when I make a mess of something that I should have been more careful about, I boldly come before God because of who I am in Christ Jesus. I continue to declare that I am blessed, and even in this situation, the blessing has no other choice other than to manifest itself. I used the example of a car so that everyone can understand the meaning of what I am trying to say. Please do not limit God's blessings to material things. Ephesians 1:3 says that we have been blessed with every spiritual blessing in the heavenly places. God's spiritual blessings include our provision, but these are not the focus of the New Covenant as I will show you later.

As I have taught this to people in different parts of the world, I have encountered something very strange. People have been so accustomed to religious phrases and Old Covenant thinking that as we end a conversation and say good-bye, they do not know what to say to me anymore. A pastor recently said to me, "You don't want me to say to you 'God bless you' anymore, so now I don't know how to say good-bye to you." With a smile on my face, I said, "Every non-Christian knows how to do that." What went wrong that we have become so strangely religious? I told him, "You could simply say, 'Good-bye,' or if you really have to say something nice and religious, you could say, 'Good-bye, you blessed son of God.'"

Endnote

1. *makrothumia,* "patience, long-suffering"; Strong's #3115; http://biblehub.com/greek/3115.htm; accessed 19 June 2017.

Chapter 20

Punishment, Discipline, and Consequences

These three things—punishment, discipline, and consequences—are widely misunderstood when people begin to walk in the New Covenant. It is very important that we distinguish between them as they can cause confusion and even a mess in our lives otherwise. Before I explain them to you, I want to talk a little more about God-facts and another important truth.

More "God-Facts," Same Principle

I will now give you a number of God-facts to which the same principle that we have just established applies. Do not ask God for them; rather, thank Him for them and declare that they are already yours, firmly believing that because of the New Covenant they belong to you. Do not treat them as promises, but as God-facts with a complete assurance of faith. Only appropriating faith will let us experience what belongs to us already. Do not move them into the distant, unreachable future by treating them as promises of God. Do not look at them as something God will give you based on His faithfulness, but as something God has already given you based on His covenant.

I would remind you yet again that a covenant is a legal bond between two parties, which clearly outlines how they must relate to each other. God bound Himself to you by an eternal covenant, and He cannot violate it; otherwise, He would violate His righteous nature, which defines Him as God, and then He would not be God anymore. By violating His covenant, He would self-destruct. Look at these God-facts (all the italics are my emphasis):

> •You have been chosen, according to Ephesians 1:4: "Just as *He chose* us in Him before the foundation of the world, that we should be holy and without blame before Him in love." Since it is a God-fact, you can never be rejected again.

•You have obtained an inheritance,
  according to Ephesians 1:11:
  "In Him also we *have obtained*
  an inheritance, being
  predestined according to the
  purpose of Him who works
  all things according to the
  counsel of His will."
  Therefore, your future is
  secure.

•You are complete in Him, according
  to Colossians 2:10: "And you
  are complete *in Him,* who is
  the head of all principality and
  power." Therefore, there is
  no more room for insecurity.

•You have been justified, according
  to Romans 5:1: "Therefore,
  having been justified by faith,
  we have peace with God
  through our Lord Jesus Christ."
  Therefore, between God and
  you, everything is ok.

- You have been reconciled, according to 2 Corinthians 5:18: "Now all things are of God, who *has reconciled us* to Himself *through Jesus Christ.*" Therefore, God will always be on your side.
- You have been given everything that you will ever need for an abundant life, according to 2 Peter 1:2–3: "Grace and peace be multiplied to you in the knowledge of God and of Jesus our Lord, as His divine power *has given to us* all things that pertain to life and godliness, through the knowledge of Him who called us by glory and virtue." Therefore, it is impossible for you to not live a life of abundance and godliness if you activate this God-fact by appropriating faith.

There are many more New Covenant God-facts, including the following scriptures (again, the italics are my emphasis):

For the law of the Spirit of life *in Christ Jesus has made* me free from the law of sin and death.

—ROMANS 8:2

To the church of God which is at Corinth, to those *who are sanctified in Christ Jesus,* called to be saints, with all who in every place call on the name of Jesus Christ our Lord, both theirs and ours . . .

—1 CORINTHIANS 1:2

. . . and raised us up together, and made us sit together in the heavenly places *in Christ Jesus* . . .

—EPHESIANS 2:6

Now thanks be to God who always leads us in triumph *in Christ,* and through us diffuses the fragrance of His knowledge in every place.

—2 CORINTHIANS 2:14

Meditate on these carefully and take what belongs to you. Please carefully study the Bible, and ask the Holy Spirit to give you revelation. Ask Him to remove the veil from your eyes so that you will read the Bible only through the lens of the New Covenant. Find all the God-facts, which I have shown you how to detect, and begin to thank God for them. Claim them, and by appropriating faith, act like they are in your hands. In the New Covenant, prayer life should be mostly thanking, listening, meditating, and very occasionally a little asking. Unfortunately, people have interpreted Bible verses such as those directing us to ask, seek, and find through the lens of the Old Covenant.

Before I talk about punishment, discipline, and consequences, let us go back to what we said in the previous chapter, which is the second wonderful benefit of the New Covenant. Can you remember what it is? God only relates to us according to who we are in Christ. He relates to us as children, not as slaves, as "in Christ" and not as "in ourselves." Our Christian life starts with death, burial, and resurrection. As we get saved, we die to our sinful nature, are buried with Christ, and are raised up as brand-new creations in Christ Jesus. This is how God deals with us. It is the strategy of the enemy of our souls to constantly point us to our past weaknesses and failures. When he does this, we also must point out our past to him—our past, which happened about two thousand years ago, where we died, were buried, and rose to newness of life! Look at these next two verses, which show how God deals with us under the New Covenant:

> Therefore, if anyone is in Christ, he is a new creation; old things have passed away; behold, all things have become new.
>
> —2 CORINTHIANS 5:17

> For He made Him who knew no sin to be sin for us, that we might become the righteousness of God in Him.
>
> —2 CORINTHIANS 5:21

When God looks at us, He sees brand-new creations and perfectly righteous people.

Discipline, Punishment, and Consequences

These three things can be very confusing to people who are beginning to understand and walk in the New Covenant. Questions like the following puzzle many people: "How could God kill Ananias and Sapphira under the New Covenant as we see in Acts 5?" People try to convince me that sin does not matter under the New Covenant, since we are righteous, independently from what we do; God does not punish sin anymore, they say. This is only partially true. God cannot punish us anymore for our sin; however, sin still matters. We are not punished *for* our sins, but we surely are punished *by* our sins because sin is always destructive by its very nature.

Under the Old Covenant, sin was punished because God related to man based on the Law. Under the New Covenant, God only relates to us based on the sacrifice of Christ. Jesus was punished for every one of our sins, past, present, and future. We are clearly told, "There is therefore now no condemnation to those who are in Christ Jesus" (Rom. 8:1). There never can nor ever will be punishment for any sin in our lives, but you can be sure that there will be discipline.

Allow me to give you three differences between punishment and discipline. The first one we see in the character of God. In punishment, God acts as a judge, while in discipline, He acts as a father. This is clearly outlined in Hebrews 12:5–12, and I will go into detail about it later. It is very simple to understand that because of God's righteous and holy character He must punish sin. Anything else would be unjust.

Imagine that one of your loved ones get murdered before your eyes. The perpetrator gets caught and brought before court. You are there as a witness who clearly identifies the murderer and then waits for the sentence to be passed. The judge turns to the criminal and says, "I understand what you have done wrong and the terrible crime that you have committed." He then continues to say that he is compassionate, kind, full of love, and tenderhearted; therefore, he will allow the criminal to go free. You would feel cheated and angry, which is very natural. Justice always demands punishment for a crime. Since Jesus was punished for our sin, which we clearly see in Hebrews 10:10–12, God cannot act toward you anymore as a judge:

> By that will we have been sanctified through the offering of the body of Jesus Christ once for all. And every priest stands ministering daily and offering repeatedly the same sacrifices, which can never take away sins. But this Man, after He had offered one sacrifice for sins forever, sat down at the right hand of God . . .

Maybe your father punished you for the wrong things that you did, but you can be sure that God never will. Our religious mindsets and desire for self-righteousness might subconsciously want to be punished in order to ease our consciences. We must reject this.

The second difference is in the recipient. The recipients of God's punishment are His enemies, while the recipients of His discipline are His children. God does not desire for anybody to be His enemy, yet, unfortunately, many people choose to be so. We are told in Romans 5:10 that we are no longer God's enemies:

> For if when we were enemies we were reconciled to God through the death of His Son, much more, having been reconciled, we shall be saved by His life.

Since only God's enemies receive His punishment, and we are no longer enemies but children, there is now no more punishment to fear. I want you to understand that it does not say here that the ones to whom God is an enemy will get punished. God is nobody's enemy. Unfortunately, people are His enemy because they refuse His love and reject the perfect sacrifice of the cross. Imagine that you hate me with a passion and fight against me, but all I do is love you and show kindness to you. Am I your enemy? Of course, I am not your enemy, but you are mine. Scripture shows this clearly when it says that God demonstrated His love toward us when He let Jesus die while we were yet sinners (Rom. 5:8). If He had been the enemy of sinners, He would not have let Jesus die; neither would Jesus have asked, while on the cross, for forgiveness for His enemies.

The third difference between punishment and discipline is in its purpose. Punishment is punitive, while discipline is redemptive. When God disciplines His children, depending on how they respond to His discipline, it might feel like punishment to them, but you can be sure that it is not. The purpose of discipline is clearly different from that of punishment. Punishment flows from God's wrath, while discipline flows from His love. No punishment of any sinner is for his good, but for the upholding of God's righteous nature. We are told that God has no desire for the punishment of the sinner. That is why He punished Jesus for sin. Discipline has only good and redemptive purposes.

Understanding God's Discipline

If you study Hebrews 12 in the original language,

you will clearly see with what amazing love God disciplines His children. Let me clear away the fear of God's discipline for you. I love God's discipline and have pleaded with Him since I was about twelve years old to never stop disciplining me. In fact, I deeply desire His discipline daily. This might sound strange to you, but soon you will agree with me. Let me show you from the most famous passage of the New Testament how amazing God's discipline is. Hebrews 12 talks about it, but for the sake of space, we will only read verses five and six. You must pay close attention to three words, which are *chastening, rebuke,* and *scourge.*

> And you have forgotten the exhortation which speaks to you as to sons: "My son, do not despise the chastening of the LORD, nor be discouraged when you are rebuked by Him; for whom the LORD loves He chastens, and scourges every son whom He receives."

The first thing we must remember is that God will never discipline you because you get on His nerves or make Him mad or impatient with you. God will never do this. He only ever has one motive for disciplining you, which is perfect agape love. He does not think about Himself, but about you and your good. The first way He disciplines is to use His Word to correct us.

The original Greek word for *chastening* means to teach or to train using instruction and words.[1] God is doing everything He can to train you through His Word. I love His discipline when I open His Word and He speaks to me about areas of my life which need to change. I might read about not loving money, forgiving freely, or some such thing. When I read His Word and humbly submit, this is His first stage of discipline. Unfortunately, many Bibles translate this poorly and put a negative tone on His Word. Second Timothy 3:16 says,

> All Scripture is given by inspiration of God, and is profitable for doctrine, for reproof, for correction, for instruction in righteousness . . .

The original Greek word for *instruction* is the same root word that is used in Hebrews 12 and is translated as "chastening."[2] God's first way of discipline is always instruction through His Word.

Every father would love it if, when he trains his child by verbal instruction, the child would listen and obey.

The rebellious children who refuse to obey will then come under more severe pressure through God's discipline. God sees the destruction which rebellion and sin cause us, and out of His deep love for us, will use the second measure (or stage) of discipline if we will not learn through the instruction of His Word. Remember, only if we stubbornly refuse to obey and continue in stubborn disobedience will the discipline get more severe.

We have to come to a clear understanding that God's discipline has nothing to do with Him; everything is focused on us. People ask me, "If sin has been dealt with on the cross and is forgiven, then why does God still discipline us for it?" It is because He sees and knows how destructive sin is to our lives. He loves us so deeply and passionately that He does not want us to suffer the horrible consequences and destruction sin causes in our lives. On the cross, only the punishment has been removed, not the consequences, which sin always brings with it.

Repentance in the Old Covenant is very different from repentance in the New Covenant. In the Old Covenant, people sinned, which caused the anger of God to come against them because of their sin; therefore, they had to repent, looking back to the sin they committed. Under the New Covenant, it is radically different.

Let us imagine that you discover by God's first stage of discipline, through His Word, that you have sinned because you were greedy and violated the law of love. Instead of looking back to your sin and trying to fix things with God through repentance, you come boldly to Him and repent, saying, "Father, forgive me; although You have set me free from the power of greed, I have chosen not to live in generosity, and by doing so, have harmed myself." You repent forward, and choose to live generously. There is no condemnation in New Covenant repentance, but a change of mind, which causes you to live in the victory of the cross.

The next step in God's discipline will be what the Bible here translates as *rebuke*. Hebrews 12:5 says,

> And you have forgotten the exhortation, which speaks to you as to sons, "My son, do not despise the *chastening* of the LORD, nor be discouraged when you are *rebuked* by Him." (Emphasis mine)

The original Greek word for *rebuke* here means to uncover or to bring into the light.[3] If we do not listen, obey, and submit to God speaking to us through His Word, He will then begin to uncover our rebellion. I love God's discipline because I understand that when I open His Word every day it is for my instruction (discipline). I am eager to learn, submit, obey, and surrender. Be smart and respond to His loving discipline. Because if you do not, out of His deep love for you He will uncover things that you stubbornly refuse to obey.

If God has already moved onto the second level of discipline, and we still remain stubborn and rebellious, He will continue to discipline us in His infinite love. In the next stage, He will scourge us as it says in Hebrews 12:6: "For whom the LORD loves He chastens, and *scourges* every son whom He receives." (Emphasis mine)

This word here for *scourge* is used without exception in the New Testament to indicate something that causes physical pain.[4] Scripture does not say what physical pain God will inflict upon us, but I can assure you that He does so out of His deep love for us. Let me clarify this for you here. God will not cause any physical pain to you if you stumble, or if you fall into some kind of sin, or if you have weak moments. God will only go to this form of discipline if He has already spoken to you clearly through His Word regarding a certain matter. If you continually reject His instruction, because He loves you and does not want your life to be destroyed by sin, He will expose your rebellion and disobedience to bring you to your senses. Should you be full of self-righteousness, excuses, and blame shifting, and refuse to accept God's loving discipline, He will use the next and last measure (or stage) of discipline which is some form of pain that you will truly feel.

I was asked by someone who does not like the idea of God using physical punishment for His children if I would break my child's leg if my child were disobedient to which I replied that I absolutely would. They were shocked by my response, so I explained it to them. If I train my child through instruction not to run into a busy road, and my child disobeys me in whatever form of discipline I had administered, regardless of how kind and patient I had been, I might have to become sterner in my discipline.

Let us imagine that I am out somewhere with my child when suddenly he runs straight into the road; a truck is heading directly toward him, and it seems certain that it will kill my child, who keeps running blindly and stubbornly toward destruction. If the last and only option I have is to grab a huge piece of wood and throw it at my child's leg, breaking it and preventing his death, I would definitely do so.

You would not be a loving parent if you said, "Well, I am so sweet I would never break my child's leg; I would rather have him killed by a truck." Never forget that in the New Covenant there is discipline because of God's deep love for us. If I told you that because you are under the New Covenant, you do not have to worry—it does not matter how you live your life—I would not sleep well because I would have lied to you. Be smart and listen to His instruction.

Endnotes

1. *paideia,* "the rearing of a child, training, discipline"; Strong's #3809; http://biblehub.com/greek/3809.htm; accessed 19 June 2017.

2. *Ibid.*

3. *elegchó,* "to expose, convict, reprove"; Strong's #1651; http://biblehub.com/greek/1651.htm; accessed 19 June 2017.

4. *mastigoó,* "to scourge"; Strong's #3146; http://biblehub.com/greek/3146.htm; accessed 19 June 2017.

Chapter 21

The Heart of the New Covenant

Before I share my final thoughts in this book about the heart of the New Covenant, I need to explain to you the importance of understanding the consequences of choices. Because of a lack of understanding about this topic, when people suffer the consequences of their choices, they often think that God is mad at them and is disciplining them. We must learn to leave God out of the consequences of our choices; they have nothing to do with Him. Christians often blame God or the devil when they suffer the consequences of their own choices.

The New Covenant removes God's punishment from our lives as we have seen, but neither the discipline of God nor the consequences for our choices will be removed. If you jump off a building and injure yourself, God did not punish you; you suffered the consequence of your choice. If you have a sexual relationship outside of marriage and contract a sexually transmitted disease, God did not punish you. AIDS is not God's punishment of homosexuals or promiscuous people; it is a consequence of a personal choice.

If you overeat, fail to exercise, harbor resentment and bitterness, and abuse your body, and then suffer such consequences as bad health, obesity, and heart problems, it has nothing to do with God. If I were to commit adultery, God would not punish me for it as He has already punished Christ for it. However, I would surely have to carry the consequences of my own actions, which among others things could be a destroyed marriage, family life, and ministry. Paul said this beautifully in 1 Corinthians 10:23, where he tells us that it is not a question of what he is allowed to do but about what edifies:

> All things are lawful for me, but not
> all things are helpful; all things are
> lawful for me, but not all things
> edify.

If you overspend your money and live above your means and get into debt, it has nothing to do with God punishing you with poverty; you are simply suffering the consequences of your choices. If you choose to spend your time in front of the television or surfing the internet or on social media instead of studying the Bible and enjoying the presence of God, the natural consequences will be that you will have a lack of Bible knowledge and intimacy with God and a powerless ministry.

The Moral Universe

God created the universe. Since He is a God of perfect love, He created a moral universe of love. Jesus told the Pharisees, not the Christians, that the Kingdom of God was within them:

> Now when He was asked by the Pharisees when the kingdom of God would come, He answered them and said, "The kingdom of God does not come with observation; nor will they say, 'See here!' or 'See there!' For indeed, the kingdom of God is within you."
>
> —LUKE 17:20–21

It is important to notice that He never said this to Christians who were inside the Kingdom, but rather to people who were outside of it. It means that the very laws of the Kingdom of God are stamped inside every person. Since the Kingdom of God is a kingdom of love because that is the very nature of God, every time we do not walk in love, we live against ourselves. There are always consequences for not walking in harmony with this perfect universe of love. I love the saying, "When you do not know what to do, do the most loving thing."

Sometimes I think that rats are smarter than many of us. I read an article about scientists putting rats in a maze with a piece of cheese at the very end. There was only one correct way to get to the cheese. Every time a rat took a wrong turn, it would suffer a small electric shock. The rat never went the wrong way twice and eventually got to the cheese. When people keep suffering the consequences of their wrong choices, instead of learning their lessons, they often end up repeating them and then blaming God. This ultimately causes them great harm, and they are then unable to live in an intimate relationship with God.

I feel passionate about the New Covenant because I am convinced that it expresses the heart of God. I have seen terrible abuses concerning the message of the gospel of grace and the New Covenant. The internal battles that I fought before sitting down and writing this book were very intense and difficult because of the abuses I have seen. Just because the message of the New Covenant has been abused by some as a license to sin does not mean that we should now shy away from it; rather, it means that we should teach it correctly.

The Prophetic Warning

In 2 Timothy 3:1–5, the apostle Paul gave us a strong warning regarding the days we are now living in. We see this scripture fulfilled all around us as the stage is being set for the appearance of the Anti-Christ:

> But know this, that in the last days perilous times will come: for men will be lovers of themselves, lovers of money, boasters, proud, blasphemers, disobedient to parents, unthankful, unholy, unloving, unforgiving, slanderers, without self-control, brutal, despisers of good, traitors, headstrong, haughty, lovers of pleasure rather than lovers of God, having a form of godliness but denying its power. And from such people turn away!

Among this list of terrible things that Paul said would happen in the last days, three things stick out to me, which are rampant in the Church today. All three are a result of abusing the message of the New Covenant. These three are found in verses two and four, which say, "Men will be lovers of themselves, lovers of money lovers of pleasure rather than lovers of God."

More than thirty-five years ago, I was in a meeting where a friend of that great man of God and restorer of the message of faith to the Church, Kenneth Hagin, was saying that he recently was in a personal meeting with Mr. Hagin, who told him in tears that he would rather have died than witnessed how people abused his teachings about faith for selfish gain and greed. Selfish people will always abuse the truth of the Word of God for their own pleasure. Nevertheless, the New Covenant is still in the center of the heart of God, and religion, which is of the devil, is a distortion of the wonderful character of God. Therefore, I will faithfully continue to teach about the New Covenant.

The heart of the New Covenant is not blessings or things we can get from God; instead, it is relationship. Let us look at the prophetic announcement of the New Covenant in Hebrews 8:10:

> "For this is the covenant that I will make with the house of Israel after those days," says the LORD, "I will put My laws in their mind and write them on their hearts; and I will be

their God, and they shall be My people."

Here we can clearly see that the central message of the New Covenant is not the blessings, provisions, protection, health, and other wonderful things that are included in it, but our relationship with God. As God talks about the New Covenant, He says, "I will be their God, and they shall be my people." This is all about relationship.

Envision yourself as a multi-millionaire being excited about your wedding day. As your beautiful bride walks down the aisle and stands next to you while the preacher begins the ceremony, she whispers to you, "Tell him to hurry up with the ceremony because I want to go home and finally have legal access to your bank account." The pain that you would feel would be very deep. God, who so passionately loves us and has given the most costly thing—the life of His precious Son, Jesus Christ—in order to bring us into this Covenant, feels deep pain in His heart when His children abuse the New Covenant.

God's primary purpose for the New Covenant was to conquer our hearts for Himself. It is not about the things we get from Him as a benefit of this Covenant. Many Bible verses have been cleverly twisted and manipulated to change the focus of the New Covenant from the relationship to the benefits and material things.

The Original Purpose of God

Paul tells us in Colossians 1:15–16 what God's original purpose for creating man was:

> He is the image of the invisible God, the firstborn over all creation. For by Him all things were created that are in heaven and that are on earth, visible and invisible, whether thrones or dominions or principalities or powers. All things were created through Him and for Him.

The Lord never created us for our own pleasure, but, more precisely, for Himself. We exist for His pleasure; He does not exist for our pleasure. We were not created for things, but for a person, who is God. Through the New Covenant, God restores man back to his original purpose of creation, which is to live in an intimate relationship with God. Because of the nature of God, which is perfect, selfless, and kind, He will not force us into this relationship or manipulate us, but He waits voluntarily for us to choose it.

The Ultimate Deception

From the very beginning, the devil has been practicing deception, starting with Eve, which caused her to sin. Second Corinthians 11:3 talks about this:

> But I fear, lest somehow, as the serpent deceived Eve by his craftiness, so your minds may be corrupted from the simplicity that is in Christ.

We can clearly see here that the reason why Eve sinned was that she was deceived. As we look at Genesis 3:6, we see how this deception operated:

> So when the woman saw that the tree was good for food, that it was pleasant to the eyes, and a tree desirable to make one wise, she took of its fruit and ate. She also gave to her husband with her, and he ate.

The devil got her to believe that there was pleasure outside of God. God had already given her everything that she needed to have an amazing life. As she listened to the voice of the evil one, she began to believe that something was being withheld from her that would bring her pleasure. It is deception to believe that we can find satisfaction outside of our relationship with God.

It is my belief that there is an ultimate deception, which is to believe that grace and the New Covenant are the means of getting things that will give us satisfaction beyond what we can find in our relationship with God. Do you remember the three things Paul talked about? They are love of self, love of money, and love of pleasure. With a weeping heart that senses God's own pain, I beg you, do not abuse the wonderful New Covenant for self, money, or pleasure. Understand that the New Covenant wants you to surrender to the God who loves you by entering and remaining in an intimate heart relationship with God. All the benefits will be yours, and you will learn to access them by faith.

Finding Pleasure Inside and Outside

People who have fallen for the ultimate deception, which is abusing the New Covenant for self, money, or pleasure, try to find pleasure either inside or outside. Let me explain this statement to you. People have walked away from the Church to find pleasure in the world. These are the ones who are very obviously abusing the New Covenant, trying to find pleasure outside of the Church.

There are others, who for various reasons, do not leave the Church but have still fallen for the ultimate deception. They now try to find pleasure inside the Church, which is much more dangerous because of its subtlety. They can quote you many Bible verses to prove that their way of living is right and approved of by God. God is a heart-God and relates to us from His heart to our hearts as we see in Hebrews 8:10–11:

> "For this is the covenant that I will make with the house of Israel after those days," says the LORD, "I will put My laws in their mind and write them on their hearts; and I will be their God, and they shall be My

people. None of them shall teach his neighbor, and none his brother, saying, 'Know the LORD,' for all shall know Me, from the least of them to the greatest of them."

We can take a very simple test to see if we have fallen for this deception or not. Look honestly at your life and analyze the things that you are asking for or claiming from God. It may be health, provision, restoration of relationship or ministry, or any other thing. Then honestly look into your heart and determine why you desire these specific things. If the answer is anything other than "for the glory of God," it is the wrong answer. Paul told us that everything we do we should do for the glory of the Lord (1 Cor. 10: 31).

I have witnessed people who start out serving the Lord with passion and fervency because the New Covenant conquered their hearts. Years later, very subtly, their ministry has become more important than their intimacy with God. We must not allow such deception into our lives. Just as God desires intimacy with us, we also must desire it with Him. I came to understand that this is a beautiful cycle.

Desire is a choice. Choices follow that desire, which in turn causes us to desire even more. In the natural, this is easy to detect. We make a choice to desire more food than we need. Once we open our heart by choice for this desire, choices for more food continue to control our appetites. The more we eat, the more we want. Before we notice it, we are obese. You can apply this to money, material things, and sexual behaviors—in fact, to almost anything.

Let us apply this to the New Covenant, which expresses God's desire for intimacy with us. God made the choice to desire us, the choice of sacrificing His precious Son followed, and now His desire for us is insatiable. Now it is our time to respond to Him. You must choose to desire Him. After you make this choice to desire Him, natural choices, like spending time with Him and surrendering to Him fully will follow. This, in turn, will increase your desire for Him, and you are in a wonderful cycle of the New Covenant love-relationship.

When the New Testament talks about desire, it does not talk about a feeling, but, more aptly, a choice. Unfortunately, in the minds of many Christians, desire is associated with feelings, rather than with choice. Two scriptures which show very clearly that desire is a choice rather than a feeling are 1 Corinthians 14:1 and 1 Peter 2:2. In both of these verses, the word *desire* is written in the active voice, which means it is something we do rather than something we feel.

> Pursue love, and ~~desire~~ spiritual gifts, but especially that you may prophesy.
> —1 CORINTHIANS 14:1

> . . . as newborn babes, desire the pure milk of the word that you may grow thereby . . .
> —1 PETER 2:2

I hope the pages of this book have awakened a longing in you to walk in the New Covenant. If it has been helpful to you, please keep me in your prayers and recommend it to others. You can also follow me on Facebook. It is my prayer that you would live intimately with the Lord enjoying the New Covenant. Never forget . . .

"It is finished!"

Made in the USA
San Bernardino, CA
07 December 2019

61050772R00162